U. S. Consulate General, Stuttgart, Germany

Date May 6, 1946

1. This is to certify that Inge Lise AUERBACHER , born at
(name in full)

German , Kippenheim , Baden , on 31st
(country) (town) (district) (day)

of December , 1934 , Female , Single , intends to immigrate to
(month) (year) (sex) (marital status)

_____ , intends to immigrate to
(given & maiden name of wife)

United States

2. He (she) will be accompanied by Berthold AUERBACHER, born June 13, 1898, at Kippen-
(Here list all family members by name, heim, Germany, (father) German
birthplace & date, together with citizen-
ship of each) Regina AUERBACHER, born August 1st, 1905 at

Jebenhausen, Germany, (mother) German

3. His (her) occupation is Child

4. DESCRIPTION

Height 4 ft. 11 in.

Hair Dk. Br. Eyes Brown

Distinguishing marks or features:

None

Inge Lise Auerbacher

(Signature) of father

5. He (she) solemnly declares that he has never committed nor has he been convicted of
any crime except as follows No exceptions

6. He is unable to produce birth certificate, marriage license, divorce papers and / or police
record for the following reason(s) _____

I hereby certify, to the best of my knowledge and belief, that the above
statements, photograph and description of are true and correct.

Signature of applicant

J.T. Rogers (Signature of consul)

May 6, 1946
(Date)

Certificate of Identity in lieu of Passport.

ADMITTED PERMANENT

MAY 24 1946

, 19

(Immigrant Inspector)

Station New York, N. Y.

Date

*Official stamp on
arrival in America,
May 24, 1946.*

Beyond the Yellow Star
To America

by
Inge Auerbacher

With photographs from the author's collection.

Royal Fireworks Press
Unionville, New York
Toronto, Ontario

I dedicate this book to:

*My beloved parents, whose healing touch nursed me back
to good health, and gave me life.*

*America, the country that gave me safety, love, respect,
and a chance to make my dreams come true.*

*All immigrants who continue to both bring and find heart,
imagination, and energy in their adopted
American homeland.*

Royal Fireworks Press   Royal Fireworks Press
First Avenue   78 Biddeford Avenue
Unionville, NY 10988   Downsview, Ontario
(914) 726-3333   M3H 1K4 Canada
FAX: (914) 726-3824   FAX: (416) 633-3010

ISBN: 0-88092-252-4   Paperback.
        0-88092-253-2   Library Binding.
          BT 7.9916.87 2196
Library of Congress Catalog Card Number: 94-69460

Printed in the United States of America by the Royal Fireworks
Press of Unionville, New York.

Beyond the Yellow Star
To America

Acknowledgements

My most heartfelt thanks go to my wonderful parents who never stopped believing in me.

I am immensely indebted to my publishers Myrna and Tom Kemnitz for their warmth, guidance, and intellect.

I would like to express my sincere thanks to the following; without their friendship, support, and inspiration this book would have not been completed:

Elie Wiesel, Andrew W. Mellon Professor in the Humanities at Boston University, and Nobel Prize Winner.

Sister Rose Thering, O.P., PhD., Executive Director of the National Christian Leadership Conference For Israel.

Randolph L. Braham, Distinguished Professor Emeritus of the City University of New York and the Director of the Rosenthal Institute for Holocaust Studies.

Benjamin Meed, President of the American Gathering/Federation of Jewish Holocaust Survivors.

Judith S. Kestenberg, M.D., Co-director of the International Study of Organized Persecution of Children.

Appreciation goes to the following for lending a helping hand:

Dr. Marcia Posner, Doris Gold, James and Anne Donenfeld, Jerry Jacobs, Else Bakke, Orest Dutka, Mollie Kramer, Dr. Kurt Maier, Emanuel Rund, Stewart Ain, Tim Boxer, Adam Dickter, The Simon Wiesenthal Center, the Anti-Defamation League of B'nai B'rith, The United States Holocaust Memorial Museum, the helpful staff of the Jackson Heights Branch of the Queens Borough Public Library System, and the Anne Frank Center U.S.A.

I am grateful for the permission to reproduce photographs from "Daily News," and the "Courtesy of the Archives of the Episcopal Church."

I am indebted to my teacher Theodor Rothschild of the Jewish School in Stuttgart, Germany for his profound influence for my love for writing, which has followed me through life, and to Hyman Ruchlis, the former Chairman of the Science Department at Bushwick High School in Brooklyn, N.Y. for introducing me to the wonderful world of science, which ultimately became by vocation.

I am thankful to Dr. Sidney Weiss, and to so many other people whose name's omission by no means lessen the measure of help they gave me in completing this book.

Contents

'Miracle Ship' Comes In

Dazed Hitler Victims Show Solemn Joy

Another "miracle ship" came to port today, its cargo of 661 refugees still dazed by the wonder of their survival of the years of horror under Hitler.

There were no cries of joy, no cheers, no singing as the S. S. Marine Perch, second ship carrying quota immigrants to arrive since war's end, docked at 12:30 at Pier 90, North River.

A cathedral hush lay like mist over the scene as the new Americans started down the gangway, their lean faces taut, half-hopeful. There was quiet, too, among more than a thousand anxious relatives and friends lining a long aisle inside the building. Banners, bearing the names of refugees they sought, bobbed above their heads.

A loud speaker called out the name of each passenger and a friend or relative came forward. Then the refugee, head bowed shyly, walked down the aisle past rows of friendly faces, and there was applause.

"New York Post," May 24, 1946.

CHAPTER ONE

The Homecoming

Spring is my favorite season. Wonderful things happen to me in the spring. Even the sound of the word is filled with energy and hope. The milestones of my childhood happened in the spring.

I will never forget the spring of 1945. I was ten years old. It was when my parents and I were liberated by the Soviet Army from Terezin, a concentration camp in Czechoslovakia, where we were imprisoned for three years between 1942 and 1945 because we were Jewish. From 1941 to 1945, a total of 140,000 Jewish people were sent to Terezin; 88,000 of them were shipped to the killing centers of the East; and 35,000 died of malnutrition or disease in Terezin. We three had survived the dark days of horror that enveloped a continent; the brutal force of Nazism, which threatened to spread throughout the world and destroy it. This awful power finally was defeated by the Allied Armies of the United States, Great Britain and the Soviet Union.

World War II, the most terrible war in history, consumed fifty million lives. Among this total were eleven million people declared "enemies" of the Nazi state—Germany. They were murdered by Adolf Hitler's henchmen through starvation, gassing, slave labor, and other methods of torture and cruelty. Six million of them were Jews. Two-thirds of the total Jewish population of Europe had been killed. This dreadful period is now called "The Holocaust."

The air-raid sirens no longer screamed their warning of impending danger of falling bombs from the skies in Europe. But, the war still raged in Japan. President Truman of the United States, after much soul-searching, ordered the first use of atomic bombs. They were dropped on two Japanese cities—Hiroshima and Nagasaki. The bombs killed thousands of people outright, maimed thousands of others and produced much destruction. Soon afterwards, on September 2, 1945, Japan surrendered. After six long years, World War II was finally over.

The world sighed deeply: "Thank God it's over!" Even the flowers bloomed with brighter colors. Rain drops had a more gentle touch, and the birds chirped with hardier throats. Nature itself felt liberated.

I was given the gift of life, but many of my friends had their innocent young lives snuffed out, because they were Jews. One and a half million Jewish children were killed in the Nazi Holocaust.

I tore the yellow Star of David with the word "Jude," meaning Jew in German, off my clothes on May 8, 1945, when Terezin was liberated. I, of course, felt tremendous relief. On that day I was reborn. May 8 became my second birthday. On September 1, 1941, Jews in Germany were ordered to sew this symbol on their clothes as a distinguishing mark, and that badge of shame had in German eyes branded me for four years as an outcast to society.

Some weeks after our liberation, a bus arrived from Stuttgart, Germany to pick up the small group of survivors from the state of Wuerttemberg. Out of our original transport of about twelve-hundred people, there were only thirteen survivors! My mother,my father, and I were among the tiny group.

We were brought to the displaced persons' camp in Stuttgart, a temporary facility, which had been prepared to house returning Jewish refugees. I did not meet any other children in this large building, and I soon felt lonely, surrounded only by adults. We arrived with very little clothing and no money to a war-ravaged Germany, the country of our birth. It had been my family's home for hundreds of years. I overheard my parent's conversation about leaving this place after only one week. "We must try to begin a new life again," Papa whispered to Mama. Papa was always the one with hope and optimism; even during the darkest days of our imprisonment. He would try to calm our fears: "Don't worry, we'll get through this, and we'll have our own car again," he would say. Sometimes, when the hunger pangs became too strong, these words were not convincing. And there were constant rumors of our deportation to another camp in the East where conditions were presumed to be worse.

I was happy with my parent's decision to leave the displaced persons' camp, where everyone looked so sad, and people were quick to argue with one another. Most people seemed constantly on edge, often crying and speaking about missing members of their families. They had little hope of finding anyone alive. They made me feel uneasy.

However, we were given an ample supply of food, and each dish tasted like the best one I had ever eaten. I asked for second helpings, even though I felt full. I watched others do the same. Food was still a luxury to me. I felt that by over-eating, I could stockpile the food...just in case conditions would suddenly change. I had grown quite a bit during the three years at Terezin, and I looked thin for my height.

When the day of our departure from this first temporary home finally came, I was excited and relieved. I wanted to leave the past behind, and just be a normal child again. The three of us held on to each other as we walked out the door. My heart was racing, and I suddenly felt anxious. My throat was dry and I had trouble swallowing. I was breathing fast. *I hope that this is not a joke, and the Nazis will come back and return us to Terezin and kill us.* As soon as these thoughts came, I tried hard to block them out. *No, no, I have to forget. I am now free, and that is how it must stay.* I looked at my parents. Their faces seemed to show fright. *Did these same thoughts cross their minds?* I wondered. I held my doll Marlene tightly in my arms and whispered to her, "Don't worry, I'll never leave you." She had been a gift from my grandmother when I was two years old, and she was my most prized possession. I protested loudly when a Nazi guard tried to take her from me. When I arrived at Terezin, I was allowed to keep only Marlene and the clothes I wore. I promised that I would always try to protect and guard her with my life. It was Marlene to whom I turned when I felt sad, she heard my sobs and felt my tears.

We still wore the same shabby clothes that were issued to us at Terezin. Papa had been somewhat over-weight before our imprisonment. Now, his face looked thin and his clothes hung loosely on him. His dark-brown eyes had always sparkled: now they looked empty and sad. He had lost most of the hair on his head, and his cheekbones protruded from a previously full, round face. He walked slowly, as if he had to replenish his energy with each new step. Mama also had lost much weight. Her forehead was crossed with worry lines. At Terezin, she had worked hard as a nurse, taking care of the very ill, elderly, female inmates.

◆ ◆ ◆

After we left the displaced persons' camp in Stuttgart, we did not return to live in my, and my father's birthplace, Kippenheim, a village in Southern Germany. We chose instead the village of Jebenhausen, my mother's hometown, located a few hundred miles away. Jebenhausen was familiar to me, since we had lived with my maternal grandparents in 1939.

Papa's parents had died a few years before his marriage to Mama. My grandparents were the only remaining Jewish family in this village of one thousand inhabitants. Grandpa made his living by buying and selling cattle, an occupation practiced by many Jews in Southern Germany. Papa's father had also been a cattle dealer, and he bought and sold skins and hides. Both families owned large houses, and belonged to the middle class.

I was very happy in Jebenhausen. Although they knew I was Jewish, the Christian children had treated me with kindness at a time when Hitler's venom of anti-Jewish propaganda was quickly spreading throughout Germany.

Our stay in Jebenhausen was meant to be short. We sold our house in Kippenheim at a cheap price and packed our belongings. We had plans to leave Germany to get out of harm's way, when the situation became too threatening for the Jews. Our destination was either Brazil or the United States. Two of Papa's four sisters and their families had found their way to Brazil. Mama's only brother and wife had left for the United States. Papa had hesitated in making plans for our departure from Germany. He was very patriotic and loved the country of his birth, assuming that nothing would happen to us because of his military service and loyalty to Germany. "These times will change again. All this will blow over soon. Hitler is a crazy man and the German people will see the light," he always reassured, when Mama pressed him for a decision to leave.

Papa was a soldier in the German army in World War I. He was only eighteen years old when an enemy bullet tore through his right shoulder and wounded him badly. He was decorated with the Iron Cross for his bravery in the service of his country.

Grandpa died soon after our arrival in Jebenhausen from the effects of mistreatment he had suffered during his short stay in the Dachau concentration camp in Germany in November of 1938. This was during the "Kristallnacht" or the Night of Broken Glass episode; the purge against the Jews, which heralded the beginning of the Nazi Holocaust. Papa also spent a short time in Dachau. His textile business was taken from him by the Nazis in 1939. It was only after these episodes that Papa decided we must leave Germany. He realized that the Nazis would have no consideration for any Jew, even if he was a decorated disabled war veteran. All my parent's efforts to leave Germany failed when the doors to the free world closed. We were forced to endure the brutality of the Nazi regime.

Our decision to return to Jebenhausen after our incarceration was based on our hopes of finding Grandma there. She had been deported at the end of 1941 to the Riga concentration camp in Latvia. We were informed by the few returning survivors from Riga that most of the people were shot in a forest near the camp. Older inmates and children had no chance for survival. Grandma was most likely among the victims. This information was not new to us. Soon after Grandma's deportation, one of the towns-people from Jebenhausen came to our house late at night with the news that he just came from Riga, where he was stationed as a soldier. He was not wearing his Army uniform, and seemed to be in a rush. He spoke quickly, without any emotion, "I saw your mother binding straw." Our hearts jumped. Mama was full of questions, "Did you speak to her? How did she look?" He bowed his head and continued to speak in a whisper. We were not prepared for what was to follow. "They're all dead! They shot most of them in a forest. That's what I heard from another soldier." He did not wait for our response, and left, slamming the door behind him. My parents remained motionless and silent in disbelief, trying to block out the news they had just heard. The words sunk in after a minute, and I saw Papa place his arm around Mama.

I was told to leave the room, but I remained standing behind the door. I heard loud sobs. Mama was crying hysterically. I heard her say, "It can't be true! She must still be alive...only animals are shot...not decent human beings." I touched my face, it was wet with tears. I always became sick to my stomach when I was scared or nervous. Now, this same awful feeling over-came me. "Oh God," I said in a whisper, "Please don't let me get sick. I have to be strong for Mama. Oh God, please let this awful story be untrue, and bring Grandma back to us. I miss her so." I ran to the bathroom and threw up.

Mama soon knew that there was something wrong with me, for when she called me, and there was no response. She found me in the bathroom and realized my condition. She spoke softly, "You heard, you heard. You poor child." Mama stroked my hair, and took me in her arms. It felt safe to be cradled again in her warm embrace. I wanted to stay there forever. Here no one would dare hurt me. I remained within her warm arms for a long time…until I felt whole again.

I remember, after Grandma was taken away I cried myself to sleep every night. I covered my head with the warm down comforter, hoping that it would block out the sound of my sobs, that my parents could not hear me. They both were constantly on edge, and I did not want to make them feel worse. I kept repeating to myself, "Grandma will come back, those stories must be untrue." I prayed for her safe return every night.

Mama did not want to accept the truth that Grandma did not survive the war. "Miracles do happen. There's always a chance that the stories are untrue," she kept repeating. I would have been so happy to embrace Grandma one more time.

We took the train from Stuttgart to Goeppingen, the larger neighboring town to Jebenhausen. Since there was no bus service, we walked the two miles to the village. Mama recognized several people during our walk. Some of them stared and were afraid to speak to us at first. Others were shocked and greeted us with surprised looks. "You are still alive! We thought you were dead like the rest of the Jews!" They looked at the three of us in disbelief. One man continued to speak: "Even the child is still alive! I have not seen any children come back around here. How did you manage this miracle?" Papa answered quickly, "It was luck, fate, chance or what ever you want to call it. During the last selection at Terezin for the death-camp, Auschwitz, a red circle was drawn around our names. That is the only reason we are here today. We could not do anything to prevent our deportation—no bribe, nothing! Imagine, one red circle could determine if you live or die." Papa was out of breath after he completed the story of our survival. His cheeks were crimson. There were tears in his eyes. His body trembled from the excitement of the last few moments. I had never before seen him in such a state.

We approached my grandparent's house. We knew deep in our hearts that Grandma had not survived. But, we did not want to accept this fact. The hardest thing was to enter the house without her coming to the door to greet us.

When Grandma was deported to Riga in 1941, her house was taken from us. We were ordered to move into the Jewish houses in Goeppingen. A Christian family received permission to occupy Grandma's house. The new owners of Grandma's house prepared a room for us. We finally had to accept the terrible truth that we would never see Grandma again. The villagers treated us with kindness, but we chose to leave Jebenhausen after a few weeks. We moved to Goeppingen to try to begin the slow process of rebuilding our lives.

A spacious apartment was found for us through the help of the mayor and the American Armed Forces Command stationed in Goeppingen. It had belonged to a prosperous Jewish family killed during these awful years. All our possessions had been taken away from us before our deportation to the concentration camp. My parent's bedroom set was located in a former SS officer's home. It took much convincing, before it was returned to us. My room was furnished with a bed, a dresser with large mirror, and night table. Mama made it look very cheerful by hanging some pictures on the wall.

I woke up slowly that first morning in our new apartment. The bed was large and the white sheets, light comforter, and huge pillow embraced me with their special touch. I felt as if I was floating on a large white cloud. *Was I still dreaming?* Mama had left the window partially open, and a soft summer breeze gently swayed the fluffy white curtains. It caressed my face like a soft kiss. Sunlight flooded the whole room. *What time is it? It must be awfully late,* I thought. I felt as if I had slept for days. I could hear automobile noise coming from the street. *Perhaps, it was an Army jeep or truck. The American soldiers drove so fast, and their cars made a lot of noise. Maybe, they wanted to show off their power as victors. They always seemed to be in a hurry. But why?* I thought. *The war in Europe was over; where were they rushing to?* I blinked my eyes and rubbed my face to try to get a grasp on things. I took a deep breath. The air tasted clean and fresh. Terezin had been so different with its overcrowded, dingy, and foul smelling rooms. Now, I slept in my own soft bed. In the camp we slept on the floor, or, if lucky, on double and triple-deck bunk beds.

I got out of bed and stood in front of the mirror for a short time. The reflection I saw was fuzzy. I quickly looked for my glasses, and the reflected image became clear. It was the first time in many years that I could study the face looking back at me. Mama had managed to save a small pocket mirror during our stay in Terezin. That was considered a real luxury. She let me borrow it at times; always insisting I handle it with great care. The mirror was so small that it was difficult to see my whole face.

I wondered if my looks had changed so much in a few weeks that people treated me differently now. My face was still surrounded by curly, dark-brown hair. My sight had not improved, and glasses were still in order. I stared at myself in the mirror for a long time. The face was not beautiful, but it definitely was not ugly or mean. I always hated those glasses, and thought they made me look unattractive. I saw nothing out of the ordinary. The Christian children did not look any better. Some wore glasses, too, and had dark hair like me. *Then why,* I wondered, *was there so much hatred directed at me during those awful years?*

I remained standing in front of the mirror, while other scenes came to mind. I remember looking at posters on my way to school, before being sent to Terezin. They showed ugly pictures of Jewish people; depicting them as criminals with curly hair, beady eyes, and long, hooked noses. These posters made me very angry. I was six years old, and my reading skills were still poor. But, I was able to read the slogans on the bottom of each picture: "These are Jews, they are your enemy!" I did not look like that, neither did my parents, or any of our friends. I thought that the Christians must have different eyes to make Jews look so terrible to them. Then I recalled my best friend Elisabeth who was a Christian. She never told me that I looked like a monster. I stood in front of the mirror at that time to reassure myself that I did not look like the people in the posters. *They are lying!* I told myself. From then on, I walked quickly past those posters, avoiding them. I hoped that other people would ignore them too and make them meaningless. If most Christian people would not acknowledge their presence, it would be as if they did not exist. Then they could not hurt us. But, to my disappointment, this did not happen. Many children heckled and taunted me on my way to school. They pointed to my yellow star sewn on my clothes and yelled, "You are a dirty Jew!"

I reminded myself, *This is 1945 not 1941.* I moved away from the mirror, shrugged my shoulders and sighed. *People are really strange. One day they hate you because you are a Jew; the next day they want to be your friend because you are a Jew. I am totally confused. Now, it's getting late, I'd better get dressed.*

I took a walk and investigated our new surroundings after lunch. Our five room apartment was on the ground floor of a two-family house on Fruehlingstrasse, "Spring Street" in German. I thought, *What an appropriate street name for our new address and new home!* Further down the street were some bombed-out houses. One looked like an open doll house. The front had been blown away. It looked like an open wound with its exposed steel girders. It was easy to identify some of the rooms. In one, the kitchen stove was still intact. In another, all the structures of a bathroom were visible. Pictures hung at an angle in what must have been a living or dining room. A few of the rooms still had colorful wallpaper on their remaining walls.

I saw deep craters and buildings hollowed to shells where homes once stood. Bombs and explosions had burned and crumbled the structures to their foundations. *How strange*, I thought, *that part of the street was not touched by the war, while the other half was in destruction.* Goeppingen, with a population of about 50,000, was not as severely bombed as were many other German cities. I was surprised that the Allies did not target Goeppingen's many factories even though many of them must have been involved in the war effort.

What could have gone through the minds of the planes' flight crew as they discharged their cargo of deadly bombs on intended targets, but many times also on innocent human beings? Surely, many of them had children and families, and were not born murderers, rather good and decent human beings. How awful, that in war, killing and destruction became a mere job to be completed!

I felt a strange gnawing sensation in the pit of my stomach. I had mixed feelings after seeing the ruined houses. It must have been frightening to sit for hours in the air-raid shelters located in the basement of each house, hoping and praying for safety. Then a bomb would hit the house, set it aflame, and in many instances one's family be crushed by the crumbling concrete and steel. Did anyone survive, where were these people now? I felt sorry for the dead people. I also felt anger. Why did the German people blindly follow a madman like Hitler into this awful war that brought so much pain and destruction to so many people? "The German people deserved all this destruction," I mumbled to myself. "No punishment is enough for the evil these people brought on all of us." But, as soon as these words crossed my lips, a warning voice rose in me. *How dare you think such thoughts. Feel ashamed! Your parents did not instill such ideas in you! They always reminded you that when you wish bad things for others, there was a chance those wishes would come back to hurt you.*

How did my parents feel about the Germans? They never discussed it with me. I never heard them speak in front of me about any bad feelings they had for the German people, or what they might do to them to make them pay for their crimes. I remember hearing survivors in the displaced persons' camp screaming, "They all should die! They must be punished for their crimes! They are murderers!" Tears rolled down their pale faces then, while they continued speaking softly in what sounded almost like a prayer, "Where is Mama, Papa, my children, Oh God, God, what have they done to them!"

Surely, my parents discussed their feelings when I was not around. Since our return from Terezin, I can recall only one incident when Mama showed her feelings toward the Germans. It was on the first morning after our arrival in Jebenhausen, when the milk cart was pulled through the village. We were awakened by loud chatter. The cart had stopped in front of my grandparent's house. We looked out of the window and saw women surrounding the cart. Each one held a small, empty metal can, which soon was filled with the precious liquid running from a spout of a larger can. Mama hesitated. She had no money to pay for the milk. Papa encouraged her to join the women and get her share of milk. He said, "Necessity makes you strong." Mama heeded his advice and joined the crowd of women at the milk cart. The owner of the milk cart remembered her, and offered to give her the milk without payment. Mama thanked her over and over again. She was embarrassed to accept anything without paying immediately for it. Never in her life had she been in such a predicament. Tears filled her eyes as she promised to repay the milk cart lady as soon as we had some money. "Please forget it, just accept it as a small gift for your little girl," replied the chubby lady, while wiping her sticky wet hands on her apron. Her face glowed with warmth and she smiled a broad smile that showed her missing one front tooth.

A woman suddenly raced up to Mama at the milk cart. She wanted to greet and shake hands with her. She was a former neighbor, who had been very active in the Nazi Party and had become especially hateful toward Jews. She was smiling and full of warmth, as if nothing bad had occurred during the past years. Mama looked deep into her eyes, and spoke to her in a steady voice that all the remaining customers could hear. "You didn't know us in those dark days. You may be in full view to me now, but my eyes don't see you. I have no use for the likes of you! I will not shake your hand!" All eyes followed Mama as she walked back into our house.

Germany had been one of the most advanced industrial and cultured countries of the world. How could so many seemingly good and decent people become so evil? I had no answer, and anyway that was something for the grownups to discuss. Papa always said, "Politics are not meant for children to discuss."

I walked further and saw boys and girls playing on a mountain of rubble made from the charred ruins of bombed houses. They stopped their play as I came closer, and looked at me with curiosity. The group of six children came nearer and surrounded me. At first we stared at each other, but soon one of the girls broke the silence. "You must be new here, where do you live?" she asked. The others continued before I could answer, "What's your name? How old are you? Where did you come from?" I shyly answered some of the questions, but avoided others. It was enough to satisfy their curiosity. I did not reveal to them that I was recently liberated from a concentration camp, and that I was Jewish. I had been cautioned by my parents before the camp years to avoid revealing my Jewish identity to strangers, since it could cause problems for me. I still felt fearful, even though I knew that things were different now, and I was no longer in danger.

I remembered just in time that I had promised my parents to be home by five o'clock. The children invited me to join them the following day. I was happy that they liked me. I thought, *Would they still like me if they knew I am Jewish? Surely, some of them were taught by their parents and teachers to hate the Jews. Perhaps, some had mistreated Jewish children.* I missed having Jewish friends, with them I could be more open. This was not possible, because I was probably the *only* Jewish child survivor of the state!

My parents had invited some Jewish-American soldiers to the house for dinner. Our home became a haven for them. They were always generous with gifts of food from their army rations, packages of coffee and chocolates. Food shortages lasted long after the war was over. Most stores had very few goods to sell. Any kind of sweets and coffee were a luxury.

I joined the children next morning. I felt happy to make new friends, and began to trust them. The two mile distance from Jebenhausen after our move to Goeppingen was too much to keep up a close friendship with Elisabeth, who was a year younger than I. We had been best of friends before my deportation to the camp, even though it was forbidden for Christians to associate with Jews. Our mothers were neighbors when they were growing up in Jebenhausen. Elisabeth was the first child I turned to after my return from the camp. We discovered that we still had things in common, although our lives had been touched by different fates. We promised to stay friends for life.

I got up early every morning to meet my new friends. We played hide and seek for hours. Woe to the child who had the unfortunate task of finding the others. Our favorite hiding places were in the bushes of a small park near my home, and behind houses. The sidewalks were covered with our chalk marks of hop-scotch patterns. These games went on for hours, until our mothers called us in for meals. Then it was off again 'till dusk.

We copied the adults, and from the street picked up partially smoked cigarettes, which had been discarded by the frivolous American soldiers. Some of the children had watched their fathers fashion this tobacco into new cigarettes. You had to have special cigarette paper; carefully place the tobacco on it, roll it into a tube, and then lick the paper to seal it. We felt grown up when we collected enough tobacco to produce one cigarette. One of the boys provided us with paper. He never told us how he had gotten it. We took turns in smoking. At first I was afraid to bring this strange smelling object to my lips. I watched the others, and soon learned the trick to smoking; doing it in secret made it seem important. I did not want to be left out and laughed at for not joining the group. I always drew quickly on the cigarette when my turn came, and immediately blew the smoke out of my mouth, without even tasting it. I was afraid of what my mother would say if she detected my strange breath.

It was hard for me to believe that this new found freedom was real. *Would I wake up one day and find myself back in the concentration camp with all the restrictions and misery? Was I now like my new friends? Was it all right to act like them; to laugh, run and act silly sometimes without feeling guilty? Was it safe to be a child again? Would this new life be gone tomorrow?* I had so many questions. More answers came every day. Many mornings I woke up surprised to find myself still in my own bed, in my own room. As time went by, I began to believe that my good luck would not change; that people no longer would treat me badly because I was Jewish. I could never understand why we, the Jews, were the focus for so much hatred. I knew that Mama and Papa were decent people and never brought any harm to anyone.

Papa had his own wholesale and retail textile business before we were branded enemies of the German state. It was taken away from him in 1939 because of our Jewish heritage. Papa wanted to resume his business as soon as possible after the war, but he had no funds to buy goods. He visited some of the textile mills and met with their directors. They greeted him warmly and remembered him as a good and honest customer. Surely, some of them had shady pasts, and were members of the Nazi Party. It was now fashionable to deal with Jewish survivors who might come in handy to save their reputation as having always been decent human beings who meant no harm to anyone. Many of the factory owners wanted to befriend us, and invited us to lavish parties in their luxurious houses. My parents took me along to many of them. Some of the houses looked like small castles and were surrounded by large gardens.

Most of the factories had few goods to sell, because the war interrupted their production. Raw materials were hard to get; everything had been invested in the war effort. Papa received a roll of sheet material from one factory. He was overjoyed that he was given credit, and brought it home on the back of his bicycle.

One of the rooms of our apartment was set up as an office and stock room. It was furnished with a large cutting table, desk, and shelves. Mama functioned as the secretary and book-keeper for the new business. Word soon spread to the retail store owners, hungry for goods, that Auerbacher had some things for sale. The business grew quickly, and Papa's fortune improved dramatically. One day he surprised us with a large black car. It was a Mercedes. The car looked peculiar with its stove-like contraption in the rear. Gasoline was almost impossible to come by, and all cars and trucks had a kind of stove filled with charcoal or wood as fuel to propel them. Gas was formed by their combustion, which then powered the car. Papa came home late many nights, because the car's system got clogged. This new method was not a reliable source of energy. How lucky the American soldiers were with their endless supply of gasoline. I remember the arrival of a truckload of blankets. They felt very rough, but store owners fought and offered bribes of eggs and chickens to get their share from Papa.

I never wanted the summer of 1945 to end. It felt special to be ten years old and enjoy the freedom which had been denied me for many years. My new friends were also especially energetic, and felt relieved to be finally rid of the strains of war. Now, I could run around as much as I wanted, and know that my hunger-pangs would be stilled with the delicious meals prepared by Mama and Mrs. Eckert, our newly appointed maid. At first it was strange not to be constantly warned by Mama to stop using up my energy, and get hungry. This was the case in the camp, where there was little food to stop the noises of my hungry stomach.

A private tutor was hired to help me catch up with the lost years of school. It was an almost impossible task for Miss Mann, a kind and patient white-haired, elderly lady. I had not even completed my first grade when the Jewish School in Stuttgart, an hour's train ride from where we lived, was forced to close. There was only one school in the state of Wuerttemberg that Jewish children were allowed to attend. Miss Mann's tutoring was not totally successful, since my mind was not on school work, but wanting to be at play with my friends.

When school opened I was enrolled in the fifth grade, with the provision I would also attend some fourth-grade classes. There were few textbooks available. Many of the books printed during the war years were filled with Nazi propaganda pictures, and could no longer be used. Each book had to be shared by at least two children. This made homework often hard to complete. I had some difficulty keeping up with my studies, especially in arithmetic. The class was up to fractions, when I had barely mastered addition and subtraction. I was not happy at school, although the children were friendly. Our teacher, Miss Neumeister was very strict, and her demand for perfection seemed endless.

I must confess that I enjoyed the attention and preferential treatment people gave me. I desperately wanted to believe in their sincerity. It became obvious to me that everyone tried too hard to make me feel at home again. My new friends often permitted me to keep our shared school books longer, although they knew this could jeopardize their marks. They often permitted me to win in games, overlooking my clumsiness and errors. *Were they instructed by their parents to be extra nice to the "Jewish girl" and not draw attention to their own shady pasts?* I wondered.

On the other hand, I did not want anyone to feel sorry for me, and treat me better because I was the little girl, who had survived the horrors of a concentration camp. What I really wanted was to be accepted for the person I was.

There was no change in my relationship with my parents after the war. Since I was an only child, I remained the center of their attention and lives. Papa had always been very strict with me, and his hand was still strong. He had grown up in a large family where the motto was, "Spare the rod and spoil the child." In typical German fashion, children had to be submissive at all times, or be the object of reprisal from their parents. Papa never hesitated to give me a pep-talk, or raise his voice to correct my behavior.

Mama, in contrast, had a mild temper, and always tried to smooth out my run-ins with my father, whose temper had not mellowed during the war. Mama became even more over-protective. She always had to know my where-abouts, fearing that something terrible could happen, and that we would be separated. Mama encouraged me to have "little talks" with her. She questioned me often about my relationship with my new friends, and advised me not to get into trouble and call attention to myself. These talks often angered me. I felt that I was being restrained, again. Although, deep in my heart, I knew both of my parents were only interested in my welfare to grow up and become a respected and decent human being.

Despite our good new life, my parents decided to part from Germany and its cruel past. They thought that there was no future for me there. We all felt a certain uneasiness.

Just one year after our liberation from the concentration camp, we were on the move again. We were given the opportunity to emigrate to the United States on the second boat of displaced persons leaving Germany after the war. I was not unhappy to leave school, or Germany. I felt relieved.

My hometown—Kippenheim.

22

Jebenhausen.

Inge, grandparents and parents, 1938.

Mama and Inge, 1941.

Inge and parents, 1945.

CHAPTER TWO

Out of the Storm

The spring morning of May 24, 1946 was very special. I had spent ten stormy days at sea on the "Marine Perch," an American troop transport ship. The sun was rising. I was eleven years old. I slept poorly through the night in anticipation of the coming day. "I'm in America, America!" I could barely believe my words. My heart pounded ever so quickly—thump, thump, racing faster by the second.

The island of Manhattan was before me. Mama and Papa stood beside me on the ship's deck. Their faces were lined with the troublesome years of the past. Mama was forty and Papa forty-seven years old. They both seemed deep in thought. I am sure they had many questions. "What would await them in this strange new land? Could they gather their strength and begin anew?"

I had overheard my parents speak with much excitement in their voices the night before our departure. Mama showed much concern over their decision to leave all behind that they had worked for the past few months. Life was good now. Was it really wise to be on the move so soon again? Who would give us some help? What kind of work could they find? What was America really like? Perhaps, the American soldiers, who visited us exaggerated in their description of America as the land of endless opportunities. Suppose, we would face hard times. The soldiers always said, "You'll make it in the States, you have what it takes. Don't stay in Germany; leave the past behind. Give your child a new

25

chance at life!" All this advice convinced my parents to make their decision that Germany was no longer our home. The word America was repeated over and over again. It sounded as if a poem was recited. "America means hope. America is a better life. America is a safe place." I heard Papa raise his voice, "You'll see, we'll do fine over there; trust me. I'll show them what a good businessman can do." Mama was not fully convinced.

My fingers traced the outline of the Manhattan skyline. Never had I seen such tall buildings. How far away was my little village of Kippenheim now? From afar I could see strange movements on the streets. Cars looked like ants moving to and fro.

It seemed an eternity ago that we left Goeppingen and were on our way by truck to a small town outside of Stuttgart. Here we were placed in a small house together with other survivors on their way to America. I was very excited and filled with anticipation for the long journey by boat across the Atlantic Ocean. Then fear suddenly gripped me and I was panic-stricken. *What if there was a fire on the ship? I did not know how to swim, and would surely drown.* I felt dizzy, and everything began to whirl around me. My stomach was in an uproar. I calmed myself just in time before I would have vomited. *All these thoughts are silly,* I silently thought to myself. I had spoken about my fears to Mama. She had reassured me that the captain of the ship had complete responsibility for our lives. If we faced the danger of sinking, he would guide us to safety in lifeboats. Her words never completely convinced me. "What, if the captain became suddenly ill, and he was unable to give proper orders?" I asked. The thought of such deep water still frightened me. Warnings kept me straight. *You must be brave! You must be brave!* I thought.

We were brought by trucks to the train station in Stuttgart. We were in a happy mood, and talked loudly with each other. I could not understand most conversations, since very few people spoke German. Here and there, I picked up a few words of Yiddish, a language with some similarity to German, spoken by many Jews from eastern Europe. Again, there were no other children in this group.

Suddenly, there was complete silence. All eyes were fixed on the train in the station. I looked at my parents and the other survivors. All eyes filled with terror. Before us stood a freight train. *Were the Germans tricking us? Would this train really take us away from here?* These cattle cars represented death. The Nazis used such trains to transport victims to death camps. Perhaps, this very train was used in the past to carry many of us to hell. I vaguely heard Papa say, "How times change, a train of death becomes a train to a new life." We climbed, reluctantly, into the open cattle cars.

Since World War II had ended only a year before, life and conditions in Germany were still not normal. Passenger trains were scarce. President Harry S. Truman had opened the doors of America to the few Jews who had survived Hitler's hell in Europe. Our good friends Mr. and Mrs. Elkan from Jebenhausen came to see us off at the Stuttgart Railroad Station. They brought with them farewell gifts. Mama and I received dark-blue woolen sweaters which were lovingly hand-embroidered with alpine flowers by Mrs. Elkan. The Elkans pleaded with us to stay in Germany, "You have such a good life now," they said. "Why do you want to leave?" Their attempt at persuasion fell on deaf ears.

The Elkans were important people in our lives, and their friendship meant a great deal to us. My parents discussed many problems with them. My grandfather became Mr. Elkan's first friend when he moved to the village of Jebenhausen to open a small knitting mill. Grandpa was a very religious man, and was drawn to Mr. Elkan because he also was Jewish. Grandpa realized soon that Mr. Elkan was a Jew only by birth, and not by conviction. This fact disappointed him. Mr. Elkan did not want to associate himself with any religion. He had married a Christian woman, who continued to practice her own religion.

Mrs. Elkan was a trained actress. Her hair had turned snow- white at a very young age. I looked at her in awe. She was very attractive and always very kind to me. There were some rare occasions when she read to me. Tears rolled down her cheeks when she reached a dramatic passage in a story. I wondered, *How was she able to cry at will?* Mama gave me the answer, "She is a real actress, and they are trained to do that." I loved movie stars and vowed, "Some day I will become as good an actress as Auntie Elkan," the name I fondly called her.

Auntie Elkan invited us over one Christmas to show us her decorated Christmas tree. She lit sparkling candles, and placed each one in a holder on the tree. It looked so beautiful and festive. I was filled with envy. "Why were we not permitted to have such a tree at home?" I tearfully confronted my parents that same evening. They responded that, "We Jews also have beautiful holidays. Be proud of who you are. You can always go to Auntie Elkan and look at her tree."

Mama told me that the Elkans employed her in their factory when she was a teenager. She recalled one harrowing experience upon awakening from a nightmare. "Had she forgotten to unplug the iron at the plant?" She fearfully waited for the morning to arrive. Surely, Mr. Elkan would blame her for the fire and ruin of his factory. All her fears were calmed when no one came to the house. It was only a bad dream.

Mr. Elkan was never arrested and sent to a concentration camp. He, miraculously, was over-looked. No one ever thought of him as a Jew. Perhaps, being married to a Christian was of some help. This usually did not stop the Nazis, who vowed to destroy every person with even one drop of Jewish blood.

I remember Uncle Elkan giving me my last bath in our apartment in Goeppingen before our departure to the concentration camp. My parents were busy preparing for the transport, packing the selected items allowed by the Nazi directive. The order for transport came unexpectedly, and we were given very little time to prepare for our departure. Uncle Elkan's gentle hands guided the wash cloth over my body. I was not ashamed for him to see me naked. The warm water was comforting. My parents were in such a bad mood, that I welcomed Uncle Elkan's offer. He had tears in his eyes. He must have sensed that something awful was in store for us.

♦ ♦ ♦

Someone wrote in chalk on the side of our cattle car, "God bless President Truman and America." There were few cots to sleep on in our car. One was given to me. The rest of the people slept on the floor. All of us had been used to these conditions and no one complained. At least thirty persons shared a car. One could feel an infectious, hopeful spirit among most of the passengers.

I befriended a woman who taught me a Russian folk song. Its melody still haunts me. That same woman wore a handkerchief wrapped around her wrist. As our friendship grew, she showed me a secret bracelet underneath. It was laced with precious stones. She confided in me that she had managed to buy it on the black market in Germany, and would try to sell it in America. It was her only valuable possession, and she guarded it with her life.

During the day the sliding door of our cattle car was kept open to let in fresh air. Most of the daytime I sat on the floor, in the doorway between two young men, watching the scenery drift by. Once in a while the train stopped in a station and I saw other cattle trains filled to the limit with passengers. It seemed that much of Europe was on the move with homeless people searching for new living space and new lives.

An empty bucket stood in one corner of the car, intended for our personal needs, but no one used it. The train stopped frequently and this permitted us to relieve ourselves in the open fields. The train ride took about two days. Our destination was the collection center in Bremen, which was formerly used as an Army barrack by the Germans. People from other parts of Europe joined us there.

We boarded the "Marine Perch" on May 13, 1946 at Bremerhaven. It was a cold and rainy day. The ocean was restless and violent during most of the ten day Atlantic Ocean crossing—much like what our live's had been in

Europe. All of us were survivors of a terrible period, and came under the D.P.s or Displaced Persons category. Almost all the passengers were Jewish and our stories were similar. Most had survived the concentration camps, ghettos, or were hidden by heroic Christians. My parents and I came through the Joint Distribution Committee. This Jewish agency sponsored and provided us with visas.

The "Marine Perch" belonged to a fleet of troop transport, or Liberty ships, built hastily at the height of World War II to satisfy the tremendous need to bring American soldiers to the battlefields of Europe. They were never meant to be luxury ships, but were installed with only the bare necessities to carry their human cargo to its designated destination. They sometimes lost parts or broke in half in mid ocean because of their flimsy construction. None of us knew of the possible danger that we faced sailing on such a vessel. If we had known, we would simply have to face yet another threat to our lives. Our aim was to leave the hell that was Europe in the fastest way possible.

Women and children had the privilege of occupying the upper decks with at least six persons in each cabin. Men were sent to the lower decks and slept on swinging hammocks. Needless to say, almost everyone suffered from sea sickness. The ship was very crowded, and filled with the sound of many languages. People entertained themselves by singing songs from their homelands. Some had harmonicas to accompany the others. Food was plentiful, but few of us were able to enjoy it because of the constant nausea caused by the rough seas.

Mama was a poor sailor. As soon as the boat left its berth at Bremerhaven, she felt an uncomfortable feeling in her stomach. Papa and I faired better. I wanted to show off my "good sailor" form, and in the dining room chose to get a taste of everything.

Mama stayed in the cabin much of the time, because she was sea sick a good portion of the voyage. Papa and I passed much time standing near the ship's railing watching the heaving ocean waves. Their colors were always changing, depending on the weather. Sometimes they looked green with silver caps reflecting the sunlight. At other times they were murky, churning with white foam. The scenery was monotonous, the ocean incessantly hugging an endless sky.

Any change in scenery brought outcries from the passengers. Be it another boat on the horizon, or the grey outline of a whale swimming alongside the ship.

The worst portion of our Atlantic crossing was passing through the North Sea, or English Channel, a particularly turbulent stretch of water covering the distance from Germany to England. After a few days, the White Cliffs of Dover in England came in view—a marker, we hoped that the worst turbulence was behind us. How wrong we were in our speculation.

The line of people entering the dining room became shorter with each passing day. The ocean was especially rough on about the fifth day of our voyage, and I finally succumbed to the fury of the wild sea. My recovery was quick, and I proudly asked for second helpings on the following day. I was introduced to a strange red sauce called "ketchup." I liked its spicy sweet taste, and have become addicted to it since.

It was best to leave the foul smelling cabins reeking of stale air and vomit. The outside decks were a haven for the passengers. Here one strolled aimlessly, circling the ship over and over again. The fresh, salty air was addictive, and made one feel better. I must have walked enough miles to cover the distance of the Atlantic Ocean from Germany to America. It was more interesting on deck. Here I met the other passengers. I don't remember making friends with any children.

At times, a few of the ship's crew mingled with us. I remember one kitchen aid who befriended Mama and myself. He gave us, in secret, oranges and cookies. "Put them away, or I'll get into trouble," he said. He must have done the same thing with other lucky passengers. Toward the end of our trip, word got around that he was placed under arrest for undisclosed reasons. I felt sorry for him. He had been so kind to us. I often wonder what became of him.

We arrived in the late afternoon on May 23, 1946 in the New York City Harbor. The Statue of Liberty was before us. Our captain decided to anchor the ship and start the immigration process early next morning.

All of us stayed up much of the night to watch the twinkling lights of New York City. We hoped that the bright beam of the torch from the great Lady of the Harbor was a sign of welcome for us.

The morning of May 24, 1946 was chilly. I proudly dressed myself in my favorite new dress. Mama had new clothes sewn especially for me for the journey to America. The dress had multi-colored flowers on a blue background, and a light blue coat and blue hat with red polka dots completed the outfit. I felt very special. Instructions were given by the captain about the order in which we were to leave the ship. Our turn came, and we carefully walked down the creaky, narrow gang-plank. Newspaper reporters quickly gathered around the disembarking passengers. We were still a sensation and a newsworthy story, since the "Marine Perch" was only the second displaced persons' ship from Europe that had arrived with its pitiful cargo of refugees in America after the war. Flashbulbs were exploding all around us. I was spotted by some of the reporters. There were very few children among the passengers, since most of them had died in the gas chambers of the extermination camps. Each child became a special story for the press. I was soon bombarded with questions. Mama, whose knowledge of English was better than mine came to my rescue. A few weeks before our trip to America, I was given English lessons by a private tutor. My parents hoped that this crash course would turn me instantly into an American. Unfortunately, my vocabulary was limited to a few phrases such as, "How are you? I am fine. What is your name?"

A few reporters spoke some Yiddish, which enabled them to communicate with us. They asked, "Where were you during the war? How was it possible for all three of you to survive as a family unit? Did you collaborate with the Nazis? Did you get false papers and change your identity and religion?"

"No, no!" Mama kept on repeating. "It was a miracle. My husband is a disabled German war veteran of World War I, which helped us only for a short time. We spent three years in the Terezin concentration camp in Czechoslovakia, where constant selections were made for the gas chambers in

Auschwitz. We lost thirteen members of our family. Slaughtered. My mother was sent to Riga in Latvia, where she had to dig her own grave in a forest before being shot. Almost all of my daughter Inge's schoolmates were in that same transport, and suffered the same fate. To my knowledge, Inge is the only child, who survived from the state of Wuerttemberg in Southern Germany. No Jewish child was meant to stay alive in Europe. Out of the fifteen thousand children imprisoned at Terezin, only about one hundred survived. Inge is one of them."

Finally, we entered the large reception hall. Red Cross workers were busy distributing coffee and donuts to the newcomers. We searched the crowd outside of the roped off area for a familiar face. Mama was certain that her brother and his wife would be here to greet us. They had arrived in America from Germany in the summer of 1938, just before the doors to the Free World were shut.

No one was permitted to leave the hall without first going through an immigration clearance. A Red Cross worker chaperoned me to a bathroom outside of the arrival area. On my way back, a lady caught my attention. She wore a prominent hat covered with flowers, and held a bouquet of flowers in her hand. I told Mama of this lady, and how nice she must be to welcome her relatives in this way.

After our immigration clearance, Mama recognized someone in the crowd. It was Aunt Trudl. To my surprise it was the same lady with the flowers. She had not recognized me. Eight years had passed since we last saw each other. She apologized for Uncle Karl's absence. He was unable to take a day off from work in fear of losing his job.

The large hall was a beehive of activity as long lost relatives and friends tearfully embraced each other. A man suddenly raced out of the crowd toward us. He recognized my parents. It was Aunt Trudl's cousin David, who had come to the port to see who had survived. He pressed a dollar bill into my hand and said, "This is for a good start in America."

It was like a dream, we had arrived in America. On the ship eight dollars were given to each of my parents, and five to me. My parents and I carried our possessions in three suitcases. We were ready for America.

Mr. and Mrs. Elkan.

Inge and parents, 1946.

WARSHIPTICKET
1-1-43

54633

UNITED STATES LINES COMPANY

AGENT

1.	2.	3.
4.	5.	6.

PASSENGER TICKET—(Not Transferrable)

One Class   Ship __Marine Perch__   (As agreed)

Scheduled to sail __13 May__   (Passenger to be advised) 19 __46__

At _____ (Not known) From Pier _____ (Passenger to be advised)

FROM __Bremen__ (As agreed) TO __New York__ (As agreed)

NAMES OF PASSENGERS (This Passage is subject to terms printed, typed, stamped, or written below and on back of all pages)	Sex	Age	Room	Berth	Ocean Fare $	Taxes Collected
Auerbacher Regina	F	40	A20	3	200 –	8 –
Auerbacher Inge L.	F	11	A20	2	100 –	– –

__1__ Adults, __1__ Children, ___ Quarters, ___ Infants, ___ Servants.   TOTAL OCEAN FARE $ __300 –__

Issued at __Bremen__   Head TAX __8 –__

By __Kraak__   TAX __– –__

Date __13 May 1946__

__a/c Joint__ ✓   TOTAL AMOUNT RECEIVED $ __308 –__

SPECIMEN COPY

Passenger Ticket to New York, 1946.

CHAPTER THREE

Into the Sunlight

"Welcome to America," said the Immigration official to us. We left the large arrival hall and walked through the exit into the bright sunlight. The doors closed behind us—doors that separated us from the past.

There was much movement on the street. Aunt Trudl and David informed us that there was a Long Island Railroad strike and that we, therefore, would have to take bus transportation to our Rockville Center destination on Long Island, where Uncle Karl and Aunt Trudl lived.

It was decided to first take a bus to midtown and have a snack at one of the unique American institutions—the Horn and Hardart Automat—a coin operated cafeteria.

We arrived in the heart of Manhattan. I looked up at the tall buildings that seemed to touch the sky. The store windows were overstocked with merchandise. Never had I seen such an abundance of beautiful clothes, chocolates, pastries, and other food products. What a change this was for us. The store display windows in Germany were almost empty after the war.

Passersby stared at us. We must have looked strange to them. Our conversation in German was loud and full of excitement. There was so much to talk about. Eight empty years had passed, and they had to be filled in.

We entered the Horn and Hardart Cafeteria and I received my first lesson in becoming an American. "What would you like to eat?" David asked me. The food was displayed in little glass cubicles and one had to place coins into a slot to get the food. After the lever was pushed down, the coins dropped inside, a window could be opened and the food was yours. I chose a slice of apple pie. I watched with much curiosity what the other people in the restaurant were eating. Most of them had sandwiches on their plates. They all ate very fast. I noticed the same uneasiness on the streets. Midtown Manhattan was crowded with people. Everyone was walking fast and seemed impatient. Some people bumped into each other in their haste to get somewhere.

We stayed only a short time at this eatery. Aunt Trudl told us that we would have to take the subway train to Jamaica. She guided us down a short flight of stairs to an underground wonderland. She dropped the five cent fare for each of us into a slot of a coin box. One by one we were instructed to push against the turnstile to gain entrance. We walked down another set of stairs to the train platform. I was amazed to see so many people rush around in this underground, brightly lit tunnel. Trains were moving quickly in and out making a great deal of noise. My ears hurt from their loud sound and I covered my ears with my hands to get some relief. I closed my eyes for a second to see how it would feel if suddenly all the lights went out. I shuddered with fear, and grabbed my mother's hand. More trains arrived from and then disappeared into the darkness.

Aunt Trudl said that we had to be very fast to enter the train, because the doors closed quickly. The car was brightly lit and not too crowded. We all managed to get seats. I looked out of the window; it was dark. The ride was noisy. We had to talk loudly, even shout at times to be heard by each other. Every few minutes we reached another station, where bright lights illuminated the area. New passengers came in each time. No more seats were available, and people were holding on to over-head loops and poles to steady themselves. I felt tired, and I was happy that we had seats. It was exciting to take my first ride on such an underground train. The train trip took about forty-five minutes, and then we boarded the bus to Rockville Center.

The bus was crowded because of the railroad strike. Our suitcases got in everybody's way. People stared at us and spoke in angry tones for making their ride difficult. I was struck by the different kinds of people. It was only after the war that I first saw a Black person. Papa asked, "Why are people in America chewing so much, are they eating all the time?" Aunt Trudl smiled and answered: "They are chewing gum—everybody does it here."

We arrived in Rockville Center in the late afternoon. This suburban community was less crowded, and it did not have the tall buildings of Manhattan. People seemed more relaxed. Our desination was my aunt and uncle's top floor apartment in a building of attached houses on Sunrise Highway. Most of the houses on this street had stores on the ground floor. A Fannie Farmer candy store was on the bottom of theirs.

Uncle Karl came home from work soon after our arrival. He clung to all of us in a tearful embrace of welcome. He had spent the war years as a soldier in the American Army, and fought in some of the bloodiest battles of World War II.

Their apartment was small and Aunt Trudl's father was also living there. With our arrival, the count went up to six. The quarters became very crowded. We knew this could only be a temporary living situation, before we would get into each other's way.

During the next few days friends and distant relatives, who had arrived earlier in America, came to visit us. Stories were exchanged about how each managed to leave Germany, and in this way survive. So many questions were asked about the fate of loved ones left to suffer the brutal force of Nazism. "You must forget the past and start new lives!" each person kept repeating.

All our visitors looked healthy and wore stylish clothes. They gave the impression that they were well assimilated into the American way of life. They often spoke to each other with a heavy accented and poor English; knowing that we were not able to understand much of what they were saying. It was a means of showing off to us that they had become "real Americans." They called us "green horns," a term associated with newcomers.

I heard my parent's conversation after one of these visits. "How dare they speak to us with such biting words. One can not remove the horrors of the past with the flick of a brush, and be whole again. They were sheltered here, and have no idea of what we went through. How dare they lecture to us!"

Uncle Karl and Aunt Trudl.

CHAPTER FOUR

A Different Life

The first few days in America were filled with excitement and surprise. Life was different here. There was so much of everything. I watched in disbelief as Aunt Trudl threw left-over food into the garbage. "That's how we do it in America," she said.

Aunt Trudl's father had a brother, Sam, who had arrived in America in the 1920's. He saved my aunt's and uncle's lives by obtaining visas for them in 1938, just before the doors to freedom were closed to Jews. Sam owned a successful butcher shop, and the commercial building on Sunrise Highway in which they lived.

My parents were faced with the problem of finding work. What could they both do? Papa had had his own textile business in Germany. How could he use his skills in America? They felt lost. Aunt Trudl was working as a cashier at a super market, and Uncle Karl as a textile messenger, carrying bales of goods from the cloth cutter to the sewers. He also had had his own textile business in Germany, but here he had to accept any position to earn a living. Most of my parent's friends who had arrived in America earlier were employed in simple factory jobs. This was a big change from the former middle class status they enjoyed in Germany. My parents were told, "Here, no one cares what kind of work you do; there is no stigma associated with any job, like it was in Enrope."

Many positions were available during the war here. But, in 1946, there no longer was any need for products linked with the war effort. The manpower shortage was over. Jobs were scarce, and openings were quickly filled by the returning soldiers from Europe, Africa, and the Pacific. None of my parent's friends were in a position to give them any help in their hunt for work.

I looked out of the window every night from our apartment on Sunrise Highway, and watched the blinking neon signs of the stores on this busy street with amazement. *What were they saying?* Their constant on and off motion was a way of speaking to me, "You better learn English so you can understand us!"

I was beginning to feel lonely and missed my friends from the new Germany. The war was over and the time for healing the terrible wounds inflicted on the Jewish people was beginning. The Christian children had been eager to befriend me. The hateful slogans against the Jews were suddenly dropped. I felt at once depressed for leaving my new friends behind, and excited to go on the journey to America. My friends envied me. It was also their wish to see and experience the magic of America, the land described as a place where dreams came true. America, where one could buy a million chocolate bars if one had enough money. In Europe, even if one had the means to buy special things, many items were still scarce after the war.

I was sick and tired of sitting quietly while my parents were engaged in lively conversation with visiting friends and relatives. None of them brought any children of my age along. I had had enough of looking at the piles of magazines given to me to keep me occupied. One of them was familiar.

The American soldiers always brought us copies of "Life." I had enjoyed flipping through their colorful pages, but now they were not special to me anymore. I even did not want to play with my favorite doll, Marlene. I was beginning to worry and wonder, if we would ever have our own home again. I did not feel comfortable in Rockville Center. The small apartment was crowded, and I always felt that I was in someone's way. I constantly had to excuse myself for bumping into someone. I always had to wait my turn to use the bathroom. It was bothersome and strange. I longed for our spacious apartment in Germany, and the privacy of my own room.

CHAPTER FIVE

A Visit With Uncle Max

A few days after our arrival in America, Uncle Karl encouraged Mama to telephone Uncle Max in his store in Manhattan. His voice sounded luke-warm, but he agreed to meet us.

Uncle Max came to America in the early 1900's. He was one of ten children, a brother of Papa's mother. It was a shock to the family at that time and against their wishes for anyone with potential to leave the comfortable family situation of a middle-class German Jewish home and go to this "wild and untamed" land, America. He was in his early twenties, armed with a free spirit and the love for adventure, when he arrived in New York City. He knew that if he failed in this "New World," he could always return to a comfortable life in Germany. Uncle Max built an important ceramics business during the next thirty years. His store on Fifth Avenue proudly bore the sign, "Max Weil Ceramics," and was known in the wholesale trade as a mecca for fine china and glassware. He had married an American woman. They remained childless, and they lived in a fashionable penthouse apartment on Manhattan's Westside. Needless to say, Uncle Max found "The American Dream."

Papa recalled the time when Uncle Max visited Germany to see his dying mother in 1914. It was at the outbreak of World War I. Since he still retained his German citizenship, and would have been drafted into the German Army, he was encouraged to immediately return to America.

47

Of the few relatives who had arrived before us in America, Uncle Max became the most successful. Before my parents went on a massive job hunt, they were advised to visit him first. My parent's hopes of getting help from him were not high, but Papa hoped that the years mellowed him.

Mama had written Uncle Max to help us come to America in the middle of 1937. The political situation in Germany was getting serious for Jews. Adolf Hitler became Chancellor of Germany in 1933, and his hatred against the Jews was gaining momentum. Most of our friends and relatives began searching for ways to leave Germany. Uncle Max's cold reply to Mama's letter was that America was in an economic depression and had enough unemployed workers. Our arrival in America would only make a bad situation worse.

I remember our visit with Uncle Max. We made the long trip from Rockville Center to Manhattan all by ourselves, without the company of Aunt Trudl, or Uncle Karl. We located Uncle Max's large store. It looked like a glass palace. I saw fancy sets of china and fine glassware in many colors, designs and sizes. Crystal bowls and vases were displayed to reflect light at the proper angle to best show off their intricately carved patterns. Everything seemed so fragile, and I was afraid that I would knock something over. I tried to stay away from the displays, and followed my parents to an office in the back of the store.

Uncle Max sat behind a desk. He welcomed us with what felt like a forced embrace and kiss. Papa quickly filled him in on the terrible years from 1938 to 1945. He told him that thirteen persons of the family became victims of the

Nazis. All were killed in concentration camps. Uncle Max was surprised that the three of us had survived.

Papa, after seeing that Uncle Max had such a large store took heart and asked him for a job. Papa was willing to do any kind of work. Surely, Uncle Max had use for another person to help pack the merchandise. Uncle Max's reply came instantly, "I am sorry, but all my workers belong to a labor union, and I am not allowed to hire anyone outside of the organization." He offered no other ideas for getting a job. Then, sensing our disappointment, he changed the conversation and extended an invitation to visit him, and meet his wife Helen in their home. My parents reluctantly accepted his invitation. We returned to Rockville Center in a somber mood. Papa felt ashamed that he had failed on his first try at getting a job.

My parents and I visited Uncle Max in his Central Park West apartment a week later. He lived in the San Remo, an impressive building on 74th Street. This New York City area of Manhattan is very fashionable, partly because of its nearness to Central Park, and considered by many as an oasis in New York's jungle of steel and concrete high-rise buildings. We were greeted by a doorman in uniform. He looked like a general. "Whom do you wish to visit?" he asked politely. The doorman immediately telephoned to announce us to Uncle Max, who asked us to proceed upstairs. The elevator took us to the last stop—the penthouse. We rang the bell and Uncle Max opened the door. Behind him was Aunt Helen.

It was very hard to communicate with Aunt Helen, since her knowledge of German was poor, and our English was limited. Uncle Max constantly translated one language into the other. I think he was annoyed.

We were given a tour of the spacious apartment over-looking Central Park. Uncle Max guided us from one of the rooms to an open area decorated with large potted plants. They looked like small trees. How strange, I thought, to have a garden on top of such a tall building. Lounge chairs stood between the plants. Here it was quiet and the air was fresh. I felt isolated from the noise and pollution of the city streets.

Aunt Helen invited us into her kitchen. She had prepared homemade ice cream for us. I do not remember that she served anything else. I felt uneasy in these surroundings. I have no recollection of what Uncle Max or Aunt Helen looked like. To this day they remain in my memory as unpleasant names without faces, because they treated us with little warmth and made me feel like an intruder. We came from a world Uncle Max had left behind long ago and had no desire to be part of again. We seemed to be an inconvenience to him, and were only through blood ties in his life.

"Why did you come to America and not join your sisters in Brazil?" Uncle Max asked Papa. "What do you intend to do?" *Was he afraid that we would be a burden to him?*

Uncle Max disappeared into the bedroom. I peaked in and noticed that he checked his collection of ties. He examined each tie carefully, and picked out a few. He gave these to Papa. It was time for us to leave. Papa did not look at his gift before we were on the street. All the ties looked shabby and worn. He dropped them into the nearest garbage can.

The meeting with Aunt Helen and Uncle Max was as cold as the ice cream they served. I looked at my parents. They both were in a somber mood. I had sensed some hope in their voices before this visit, but time had not softened this man with a heart of stone. My parents could not expect any help from him. They were disappointed, crushed.

We slowly made our way back to Rockville Center. Papa was ashamed to come home with the news that the relative who had become most successful in America had abandoned us.

Thoughts of impending doom jolted me like flashes of lightning. *What if Uncle Karl and Aunt Trudl got fed up with us, and threw us out of the apartment. Where would we go?* I promised myself to be extra nice to them; offer to help with household chores, and not get in their way. I thought, *I must be very careful not to mess-up the apartment, and give them a chance to complain. They must never think of me as an eleven-year old nuisance. I must never, ever, answer them back, even when I am annoyed by their remarks!*

51

CHAPTER SIX

Changing Ways

So much had happened in just the few weeks since our departure from Germany. I felt depressed and lost, and was afraid of being left alone. People spoke to me in a language that sounded like jumble. The excitement of the journey and arrival in America had worn off. Now, this wonderful new country was becoming my enemy. Would I ever make new friends again? I couldn't speak to anyone because no one spoke German here. Why did we ever come to this land?

After two weeks in Rockville Center, it was decided to send me to relatives in Jamaica, an hour's drive away. This would give my parents freedom to look for jobs, and me a chance to be with children of my own age. I welcomed the opportunity to live for a while with distant cousins. They had two children, a daughter Susie and an older son, Ernie. I hoped that this would be a good move for me, although I felt a twinge of sadness for having to be separated from my parents who would live for a while in the homes of other relatives and friends.

Our cousins lived in a two-family house on a tree-lined street in Jamaica, Queens. Ernie and Susie's father, Hugo, had his own egg distributing business. The family was financially comfortable. The mother, Kaethe, was a kind and gentle person who tried her best to make me feel like part of the family.

Cousin Susie was a year younger than I and a bundle of boundless energy. When she was only a baby, she had arrived in America together with her older brother Ernie, her parents, and maternal grandparents. This was before the terrible time in Germany began. Susie was already a "real" American and thought herself an authority on this subject. She was full of ideas to make me over.

"We have to change your hairdo. No one here wears the hair wrapped around a comb on top of the head," she said. I thought that I looked fine. Most girls my age in Germany wore their hair in this style. But, after meeting some of Susie's girlfriends, I began to agree with her. The curl on top of my head had to go.

"You look strange," she said.

My clothes also disturbed her. I did possess one "real" American dress—a red and white checked dress with puffed white sleeves that Aunt Trudl and Uncle Karl sent me after the war in Germany. It was my favorite dress and I wore it only on special occasions. I remember how thrilled I was to wear it for the first time, and show it off to my schoolmates. I was the envy of my entire class.

Susie's mother took me shopping and her friends who had children who had outgrown their clothes, brought the gently worn clothing to the house for me, "for the refugee child." I soon had a full wardrobe and began to blend into my new surroundings.

Susie introduced me to coloring books. The combination of words and pictures were my first English lessons. One of the first words I learned was "umbrella."

Everything was American-style in my cousins' home. Breakfast consisted of a glass of orange juice and a crunchy cereal swimming in a sea of milk. I had already been introduced to these foods on the ship coming to America, and now I began to like their taste.

Ernie was a few years older than I. He was quiet and studious, but also acted distant to me. Perhaps, I intruded into his life. I was afraid of him.

It was the beginning of June and school was still in session. Susie took me along to her fourth-grade class at P.S. 82 in Jamaica. Once again I felt lost and isolated. I was unable to answer the other children's questions, because of my poor English. Their stares and comments made me very uneasy. Susie seemed popular with other children and was always surrounded by many friends. She probably never sensed my feelings of insecurity and loneliness. I tried hard to learn English. The few English lessons that I had in Germany were of little help to me now. I wanted so much to be part of Susie's crowd of friends.

The worst time for me was during school recess. I could not participate in most of the games played by the children. They were not the same games that I knew from Germany. Susie tried to teach me to jump rope, but I was a failure at it. The other children soon tired of me, because of my lack of participation in their kind of play.

Our fourth-grade teacher, Mr. Chinowsky noticed me. He came over to me during some of the free class periods and tried to make me feel more at ease. Among the first things he explained to me were the different measurements used in America. No one here used the terms "meter" and "kilometer." Strange sounding names like "inch" and "mile" soon became familiar to me.

Uncle Karl patiently spent hours teaching me "American" ways, although he always appeared to be exhausted from his job. I felt proud of myself one day, when Mr. Chinowsky wanted to do a lesson on the different coin values and their sizes, the same lesson as Uncle Karl's. I told him I already knew that.

This new way of life was slowly becoming familiar to me. I could hardly believe that only two weeks had passed at my cousin's house. *Yes,* I thought *I will one day be as good an American as Susie.* I was able to speak more English every day. This encouraged me to try out each new word as often as possible. People began to respond to me. School closed soon for the summer recess. Mr. Chinowsky gave me my first report card in America. It read "SATISFACTORY." I was happy that he was pleased with my effort.

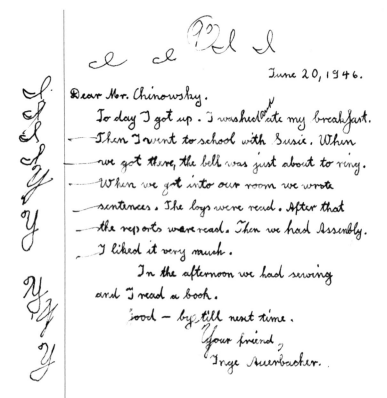

June 20, 1946.

Dear Mr. Chinowsky.

To day I got up. I washed ate my breakfast. Then I went to school with Susie. When we got there, the bell was just about to ring. When we got into our room we wrote sentences. The boys were read. After that the reports ware read. Then we had Assembly. I liked it very much.

In the afternoon we had sewing and I read a book.

Good — by till next time.

Your friend,
Inge Auerbacher.

Classroom assignment.

56

CHAPTER SEVEN

A New Home

Mama and Papa found jobs during my stay in Jamaica. Aunt Trudl's Uncle Sam, the butcher, heard of a customer's search for a couple to work as cook and butler on his relative's estate in Rye, New York. This situation was ideal for us even though the salary was small. We would no longer be a burden to anyone, and we would live together!

Mrs. Nadler, the employer picked us up by car in Rockville Center and drove us to her home. She was a petite woman. Her short blond hair was worn in a style that made her look attractive.

Rye is a wealthy community in Westchester County, about an hour's drive from New York City. The town is made up mainly of mansions surrounded by large, manicured grounds. Our destination was a big house on Plymouth Road. The garden and building were awesome. Mrs. Nadler introduced us to her three children. Two girls were nine and eight years of age, and the baby boy was less than a year old. She showed us our quarters. We met her husband in the evening. He was a manufacturer of sports clothes. Mrs. Nadler told my parents that orientation for the job and its duties would come the next day.

The servant quarters consisted of two rooms separated by a bathroom. I was given one room, while my parents settled into the other. Both rooms were sunny and were furnished with simple, but adequate furniture. My parents seemed nervous and apprehensive, hopeful that they could satisfy the demands of the position. Neither one had ever worked as a servant. While in Germany, we always employed outside help to aid my mother in caring for a large household. Mama was especially worried about cooking in the "American" style. Papa was fearful and felt degraded. He always was his own boss, managing a textile business in Germany.

We settled into our new life. Mama adjusted soon to her routine as cook and housekeeper. She quickly learned the different style of food preparation. The Nadlers had many friends and entertained a great deal. Work days were long. There were lawn parties, where the latest movies were shown. They often lasted past midnight. Both Mama and Papa had to be present at these big events. They were given very little time off.

As the days passed, I watched Papa become sad and more uncomfortable. He often dropped a fork, spoon or knife, and seemed clumsy in his work. One day I saw him cry after one of these mishaps. He felt sorry for coming to this country.

I fared better than my parents. Mrs. Nadler permitted me to play with her children and share breakfast and lunch with them. I sat proudly at the table as Mama served us our meals. My parents and I ate dinner in a separate kitchen area. I spent many hours playing with the children in their rooms. They had a children's nurse to take care of them. I was most fascinated with their record player. They often listened to the music from "Annie Get Your Gun," a musical that was playing on Broadway. I soon was able to sing most of the songs from the show. My English improved and I felt almost at home.

One day, back from a shopping trip, Mrs. Nadler came out of her car with her arms full of packages. Each of her children was given a box. To my surprise, I received one too. It was a doll. I immediately called her Beatrice, the name of the older daughter.

The children had a playhouse on the grounds. I never saw them in it. We often ran around the park that surrounded the house. A gardener made sure that the grass was always in good condition, and that the flowers were well taken care of. Sometimes we took our shoes off and ran barefoot on the green carpet, feeling the velvety cool wetness of grass beneath our feet. We felt very daring doing this. At such times, thoughts of home came racing through my mind. How wonderful it was to run barefoot through the fields on visits to my grandparent's village of Jebenhausen in Southern Germany. Grandpa was a cattle dealer, and I often joined him in the stable. I loved to be near the cows. I remember their large sad eyes. The strong stench of animal excrement did not bother me. I enjoyed helping Grandma round up her chickens at night. It was hard to imagine that the delicious chicken soup served every Friday night for the Sabbath meal came from one of them. But, that was so long ago, before all the terrible things happened to us.

One day Papa saw something jumping outside of the kitchen area. It was a frog. I begged him to catch him for me. He became my pet, Hansel. We placed him inside a glass jar with some water. We gave him a piece of wood to sit on so that he was able to get out of the water, which we thought he needed to live. We caught flies and gave him bits of meat to keep him fed, and we hoped that he was comfortable. I watched him for hours and started to feel sorry for keeping him in a prison. *Maybe, you're lonely and sad to be separated from your family,* I thought , and began to feel guilty. I certainly did not like being imprisoned in the concentration camp. But, I did not want to lose him, either.

I was happy living on the Nadler estate and playing with the children on their own playground. It was fun taking turns on the swings and jumping on the moving merry-go-round while running and pushing it to make it go faster.

Something happened one day. I felt different. All of a sudden it was no longer fun going fast on the merry-go-round. I felt an unusual tiredness, although I had slept well through the night. I took a nap. When I woke up, I still felt the same tired feeling. Maybe it was due to the cold I was harboring for a while. During our cattle car trip to the ship, I developed a minor cough. It was chilly in our car during the night, and I must have caught it at that time. Now, it had gotten worse and Mama became worried.

Mama decided to seek medical attention and spoke to Mrs. Nadler about obtaining a doctor for me. An appointment was made with the Nadler's family physician. I was examined by the doctor, but he was not satisfied with his findings and decided that I must be seen by a specialist for chest diseases. He recommended Dr. Childress, the Chief of Chest Diseases at Grasslands Hospital in Valhalla, New York.

I remember going with my parents on a bus to the large medical center. Dr. Childress was a middle-aged man. He had a pleasant and kind way of dealing with people. He examined me and told us to wait in a waiting room. It did not take very long for him to meet us there. His verdict was short and to the point, "Your daughter has pulmonary TB or tuberculosis of the lungs and must be hospitalized as soon as possible." It was as if lightning had struck my body and I felt paralyzed. I remember looking down at the black and white tile floor as I began to cry. Suddenly, I no longer saw any white tiles. Everything became a blurry, black mass. I felt like I was being sucked into a dark hole from which there was no escape, then reality came back to me. I was again part of the night from which I had so desparately tried to escape. The past flooded back in agonizing waves. Whenever I had a special problem, I would discuss it with God. I always felt that I had a unique relationship with Him, and that He would listen and do what was best for me. I know that He has to listen to millions of requests, millions of voices that hoped He would grant their large and small wishes each day. But, He would never forget me. I remember a particular incident, when I was in the concentration camp. My talk with God was filled with the urgency of our situation. Most of the people were shipped out of Terezin to an unknown destination in the fall of 1944. My best friend Ruth and her parents were among them. It seemed exciting to take a train ride, and leave the hell that was Terezin. I envied her. But, suppose it was even worse in this other place. I was very upset to be separated from Ruth, and I wanted to join her. "God," I said, "please take good care of Ruth and her parents—should we be on the next train, you decide!" Unknown to us at that time their destination was Auschwitz and death in the gas chamber. It was in one of these conversations with God that I prayed for this sickness. Children who had tuberculosis in the camp received a small food supplement. I was always hungry and this seemed an answer to my problem. All children in the camp were examined at one time for this disease. Ruth, who was even thinner than I, came out negative, while I tested positive. I was happy that my prayer was answered, and that I would become a member of this special club. Little did I know that this diagnosis could mean great harm for me, and speed up the process of being sent to Auschwitz.

But, why did I have to become sick now, just as I was beginning to get used to living in America and having such a good time? I felt well after my return home from the camp, and my previous episode with tuberculosis we hoped was a thing of the past.

Dr. Childress placed his arm around me and took us in his black car to see the children's hospital of Grasslands Hospital, where I was to be admitted. I had visions of the camp hospital, where every room was like a chamber of horrors. But, this was definitely different. Two turkey figures guarded the entrance of a pleasant looking small building. We did not enter it. Dr. Childress advised my parents to bring me there the following day. Because of all the excitement, Papa left his hat on the bus on our way back to Rye. My parents were in a state of shock.

From that time on we never again spoke of the disease by name. We called it, "The Sickness," or "It." There was still much stigma associated with tuberculosis at that time. It was considered a curse. People were afraid to be near such patients, because of its infectious capacity. It was best not to advertise it. This was not considered like any other sickness, it was associated with shame. My parents wanted to protect me from mental pain, and tried to keep the nature of my sickness a secret.

CHAPTER EIGHT

Another Prison

It was the end of July; both temperature and humidity were soaring. The combination of the two made life uncomfortable for everyone. We were in the midst of a typical New York City summer. It was hard to believe that barely two months had passed since our arrival in America. And now this blow. My parents were devastated. Who would help us? Who would pay for my hospitalization? They were in no position to pay even the reduced hospital rate of this public institution. We could not become a burden to this country, and my hospital bill would not be paid by an agency of the government. If you were not a citizen of the United States, you were responsible for the payment of your bills through private means. My parents could not expect any help from our family. They were too embarrassed to ask our distant cousins, and Uncle Karl and Aunt Trudl were in no position to share their small earnings with us. My parents were asked to approach a Jewish charitable agency for help.

Sunshine Cottage, a children's communicable disease hospital had two wards. One for polio, and Ward 200, where I was sent. It was part of a large medical center called "Grasslands Hospital," located near the town of Valhalla, in Westchester County, New York. Today, the name has been changed to "Westchester Medical Center."

Dr. Childress said, "You'll see this is a nice place, nothing like the concentration camp hospital you were in."

The next day's admitting process is a blur to me. I found myself in a hospital bed and surrounded by a screen. I was dressed in a pajama. I heard voices around me. They sounded child-like. *So, there must be more children here, but where are they?*

It must have been late in the afternoon. All the lights were turned on. I started to cry. *Where am I? No one seems to care about me.* A nurse and a young doctor finally came to my bedside. Both of them asked me many questions and wrote notes on large sheets of paper. I was able to answer most of their inquiries, since they used very simple English. They told me not to be afraid and that the screen was only a precaution. All children had to be "isolated" when admitted, to enable the doctors to evaluate each case. This protected the other children from contracting additional sicknesses that a new patient might bring to the ward. The screen would be removed after one week.

Again, I was left alone. Hours passed and I felt the need to go to the bathroom. But, the nurse had told me that under no circumstance was I to leave my bed. I was under strict bed rest now. What was I to do? I did not know the English word for bedpan, and I was too embarrassed to tell anyone of my need. I decided to wait. Perhaps, if I thought of other things the urge would go away. I tried hard, but I began to feel the pressure building and a stabbing pain in my groin. *Oh God, please don't let me have an accident,* I thought. Finally, I took heart and 'literally' translated the German word for bedpan (Nachttopf) into English, "Nurse, please give me a night pot!" The nurse looked puzzled and did not seem to have understood me. She returned with some kind of cooking utensil. "No, no this is wrong," I said. There was no more time to feel ashamed and I pointed to my bottom. She finally understood the urgent problem and ran back with a bedpan. I added another word to my English vocabulary.

Dinner was served on a tray. A young girl moved the screen slightly aside to see who was behind it. She gave me a smile and quickly ran away. I was left alone again. Soon it was night, and the ward became quiet. The experience of the day was beginning to sink in. *How long must I stay here?* I felt very depressed and homesick. *Where are my parents, and why did they leave me here alone?* I cried again, but this time in sobs. My whole body was shaking. The pain was great. *I don't want to stay here and be imprisoned again.*

I thought back to the time of the first night in the camp hospital, I was seven then. I had contracted scarlet fever during the first few weeks in the camp. My parents were not allowed to visit me. Our ward was crowded. Two children slept in each bed; some on the floor. Flies covered the walls. The room looked like a prison with its small barred windows. I waited anxiously every evening for the sound of Papa's whistle from outside of the hospital. We had our own signal to communicate with each other. When I heard it, I climbed from one bed to the other to reach one of the windows. I stood on tiptoes to be able to look out of the window and get a glimpse of my parents. Our ward was on the second floor of an old brick building. Papa and Mama looked small from where I was. If only I could jump out of the window and be with them. I yelled out to them, and we exchanged a few words.

Now I was eleven years old, but the fear and pain felt the same. I was very sad and wanted my mother to be with me. But, my parents were too far away. There would be no whistle to know that they were near and say "good night" to me. *Suppose, someone hears me crying like this. They will say that I'm a 'cry-baby'. I have to control myself. Maybe, I'll be able to sleep and I won't feel this pain anymore.* My eyes finally closed. But, it was not a peaceful sleep. I twisted and turned all night. I woke up still feeling tired and depressed.

CHAPTER NINE

We Are All The Same

Day began early in Ward 200. The nurse from the night shift made her last round and took my temperature the anal way. I had been used to sticking a thermometer under my arm and had to get used to this method. It was just before seven a.m.. The day nurses soon came on duty. *Maybe, this would be a better day for me.*

Breakfast arrived on large tray trucks by eight a.m., and was served by a special food crew. I remember one short, chubby lady, Betty Steitz. She was always full of energy. All of us were happy to see her, because she always had a smile and made us laugh. I received my tray. The juice was sour, the scrambled eggs and milk were luke-warm. Two slices of toast drenched in butter were cold and tasted oily. I was not hungry and found the entire meal distasteful. I would have been thrilled in the camp to have such a feast. And that was barely a year ago. *I must not be feeling well.* The almost-full tray was picked up later by the same food aides. Betty was disappointed with me and she said in a loud voice, "If you want to get well, you'll have to eat better."

The doctors came around nine a.m. and placed their cold stethoscopes on my chest. "Hold your breath, now breathe deeply," one said. One by one the small group of young doctors repeated this examination. They talked to each other in words that I could not understand. After they left, a paper cup filled with tomato juice and a funny looking substance on top was handed to me by the nurse. "Drink it down, it's cod liver oil and good for you," she said. I didn't know what to expect and gulped it down in one swallow. Only then did I realize what I had just swallowed. The after-taste made me nauseous and I had to use will power to keep it down in my stomach.

Then I was told that we were allowed only two visitors at a time for two hours between two and four o'clock on Sundays. That was so many days away. Would I be able to hold out that long?

Next morning I was not given breakfast. *Strange.* Later, a doctor came carrying a special kidney shaped metal pan with a long rubber tube and ice cubes in it. *What's going to happen next? Yesterday they stuck a needle into my arm to take blood and that hurt. They poked around a lot until they were satisfied.* The doctor, hurriedly said, "Just swallow this quickly and it will be over fast! This is called a gastric test, and we will analyse some fluid we take out of your stomach to see how sick you are." He gave me an ice cube and told me to suck on it, breathe deeply and swallow quickly. He pushed the tube down my nose, deeper and deeper inside. I felt it pass my throat. It was very painful and made me gag. I could hardly get my breath. *Oh God, help me, I can't stand it!* He attached a syringe to the rubber tube and pulled on the plunger to remove some fluid. Then he quickly pulled out the tube. It was over.

♦ ♦ ♦

Sunday finally arrived. Mama and Papa came to visit. *Why are they wearing funny looking white gowns over their clothes?* They explained that all visitors were required to wear gowns in order to keep us from getting diseases from outside of the hospital, and to protect them from catching ours. Presents were not allowed to be given to us directly. They were first examined by the nurses and distributed after dinner. Any kind of books, magazines and newspapers went through a sterilization procedure and it took days before we received them. I was especially interested in the comic strip sections in the "Sunday Funnies," which my parents collected and brought to me. My favorite comic strip was "Dick Tracy."

My first week was over and my isolation period ended. After the screen was removed I saw that I was in a large room with about ten other girls. Some were older, others younger. The youngest, Rose Mary, was about two years old. A swinging door-separated us from the "Boys End," where there were about ten boys. No one was older than thirteen.

I was moved from a corner on the "Girls End" of the ward to a back room with three black girls. We soon became good friends. I remember Cynthia and Vina.

When my parents came the following Sunday, they were shocked to see me in a room with black girls. They asked, "Are you not afraid of them?" I told them that there was no reason for becoming alarmed and that the girls were very nice to me. "We are all the same, they just have another skin color." Black people were hardly ever seen in Germany. In my experience, only a few entertainers whose African heritage was considered wild and exotic found their way there. I had never seen a Black person before my liberation from the concentration camp. A Black American soldier came to Terezin and we ran to look at him. I remember how a little girl fearfully shook hands with him and quickly pulled her hand away to see whether his color came off on her hand.

Papa had a surprise for me. He sneaked my pet frog Hansel into the ward. He looked so sad in his glass prison. I told my father to give him his freedom. "Don't let him feel like me, it's enough that one of us has to be cooped up."

There was more news. My parents were fired from their jobs because Mrs. Nadler found it inconvenient to have my parents absent from their work every Sunday afternoon. Mama told her it was more important for them to visit me in the hospital than to keep the position, and that they would look for other work. Papa was very unhappy in Rye. This event solved his problem.

My room-mates made friends with my parents. My parents seemed content with my companions and they smiled and waved to them as they left the room. Vina even sent my mother a postcard with wishes for her birthday on the 31st of July.

The following Sunday I was permitted to wear a dress supplied by the hospital laundry. All of us were happy to take off our pajamas. We enjoyed dressing up for our visitors, even though we were forced to stay in bed. Our uplifted spirits made us feel better.

One Sunday, Mama brought a box of home-made butter cookies. My parent's friend Charlotte, from Kippenheim, had baked them especially for me. She asked my parents to deliver them. I gave each of my room-mates one, but I hoarded the rest. I selfishly ate them at night with the hope that no one heard me chewing on the crunchy morsels. I wanted them to last a long time. My roommates did not always share all their treats with me, either. I did not feel guilty. We were even.

Very few people beside my parents came to see me. Sidney Bernstein, one of the American soldiers we met after the war, surprised me one Sunday. He came from Boston with his wife to visit. He looked so different without his Army uniform. They brought me a nice present. I felt very important, and showed off to my roommates that I had visitors from so far away. There never was a Sunday without either Papa or Mama visiting me.

Papa sometimes walked around the ward to speak to other visitors. I welcomed these pauses. It was a time that I could speak heart-to-heart with Mama, and talk to her of special things that I would only confide to her. When we were alone, Mama spoke to me about Papa's unhappiness in this new land. America was not what they had both envisioned. When she saw my face turn sad, she immediately put her arms around me and said, "Please, please forgive me! I should not worry you with those things. Just follow the doctors' orders and get well. Surely, things will change for the better, and we will be together in our own home again." Just then Papa returned to my bedside. He had a smile on his face. I welcomed the change of mood. Papa had the capacity to make anyone laugh and smile. He always had a reservoir of funny stories, and loved to talk. Mama, in contrast, was more serious. It was hard for her to laugh and be jovial. Papa was the rock of the family and was determined to be seen as the dominant figure of our household.

Although Sunday was the highlight of the week, I still felt the warmth and closeness of my parents on Monday, and I spent many hours playing with the presents they had brought me. It was a day that I could insulate myself from the reality and harshness of a hospital. I shut my ears to the cries of the other children, and created my own imaginary world that did not include rows of hospital beds, demanding nurses and callous doctors.

By Wednesday I became anxious, and counted the hours for Sunday to arrive. I often thought, *If only I could wave a magic wand and make every day Sunday. I could always be together with my parents.* Saturday was the most unbearable day. "Only one more day; I have to hold out one more day!" I repeated to myself.

Papa had hated the work at the Nadler Estate; he felt degraded, but tried with all his strength to make the best of a bad situation. He felt humiliated performing the household chores expected of him. Mama adjusted more easily to this new life. She accepted each new challenge gracefully. Now I worried about my parent's future, since they told me the news of their firing.

Betty Steitz (on left), our food aide.

Oct 4, 1946
Ward 200

Rose's are red.
Violets are blue.
Sugar is sweet.
There never will be
a sweet patient
like you
Love. Betty Steitz

From my album.

September
er.
1946,28

I wish you all the luck
in the world and may you be
happy in a American and all
your dream come true.

Love

your room mate
Cynthia Barboza.

to a Very nice
room mate Inge.

From my roommate, Cynthia.

Dec. 30, 1947

Dear Inge

yours until
lip stick stick

The higer is the mountains
The harder the breeze
The younger the couple
The tighter the squeeeze

With Love

Vina Grady

Happy Birthday
to a
very nice girl

To my
very best
friend of
Ward 200

From my roommate, Vina.

74

Inge, Mama and friends.

Inge and Mama at Sunshine Cottage. Mama is wearing white gown for protection (hospital policy).

CHAPTER TEN

A Second Chance

After my parents lost their jobs in Rye, they immediately packed their few belongings. They stood with their two suitcases outside of the mansion, not knowing where they would sleep that night. Even though Papa was very unhappy in Rye, the awful feeling of losing a job was beginning to bother him. To whom could they turn for help? They felt like defeated soldiers, who despite a heroic fight in battle face the final blow of defeat.

Mama decided to turn to Uncle Karl and Aunt Trudl, with the hope that they would be welcome in their home, again. They arrived in Rockville Center in the evening, after everyone had come home from work. They promised to go job-hunting the following morning.

The next day was fruitful. My parents went to "Self Help," a non-sectarian employment agency, set up especially to help Jewish immigrants find work. My parents were greeted with a telegram from "Self Help" with a job offer shortly after they returned from the City. A call had come to "Self Help" for a German speaking couple to assist in an old persons' home in Manhattan on West 74th Street.

My parents set up an appointment for an interview with Mr. and Mrs. Streim, the owners of the senior citizen residence. The Streims came to America in the late 1930's to escape Hitler's fury. Mr. Streim was Jewish and his wife

Christian. They liked my parents and immediately hired them.

Mama was hired as a cook and waitress. She was also required to wash and dry all the dishes after each meal. The rooms of the boarders were taken care of by another lady. Mama worked very hard, but she was happy in these surroundings. The old people treated her with respect. Most of them came from Germany and Austria to escape the Nazis in the late 1930's. Many of them were able to bring over most of their money and possessions. All of them were well-to-do and able to pay the high rates of this residence. Mama's apron pocket bulged with tip money every Friday. Many of the elderly people gave her an envelope containing a few dollars and a kind note of thanks which often read, "Because I appreciate you and your gentle way."

Papa was only required to help out with small chores like taking out the garbage. They were given a room in the basement of the brownstone building. The boiler was outside of the room. It was brutally hot in the summer. The small window gave little relief in this almost airless area and cockroaches danced across the furniture of the sparsely furnished room. My parents never complained about these unpleasant conditions. They were grateful to have a roof over their heads, and a little money.

Papa had some free time and began his own business selling plastic table-cloths and pocket books which Uncle Benny, a brother of Papa's mother, produced in his own small factory. At first, he sold them to friends and to children visiting their mother or father in the residence. He offered his wares to anyone he met. Satisfied customers recommended his products to their friends and Papa's orders

77

increased steadily. My parents seemed settled for the time being at their new West Side address. They both appeared much more relaxed when they visited me on Sundays. Mrs. Streim once sent me a box of paper-dolls. Mama told me that the Streims took much interest in my well-being, and were anxious to meet me after my release from the hospital.

CHAPTER ELEVEN

Privileges, Rules and Regulations

Sunshine Cottage was mainly staffed by student nurses, interns and resident doctors still in training. All of us became experts in recognizing which schools the nurses came from by the color of their uniforms. I recall that students from the Adelphi University Nursing School wore yellow. This rainbow of color changed frequently. There were always new faces. One particular nurse, Miss Smyth, took special interest in me and used my case history for one of her required student reports. She sent me a picture of herself after the completion of her training. There were a few male nursing students. We liked them very much.

There was also a permanent staff consisting of a head nurse, P.N.s or practical nurses, who were not permitted to distribute medicine, and licensed regular nurses. I remember a kind P.N., Miss Ouisley, the nurse Miss Mahoney, and a head nurse, Miss Cousins.

My parents bought me a radio. It became an important device for improving my English. Some of the best programs came on at night, and I listened in secret when most of the lights were turned off. One could use one's imagination better in the dark; the crime stories sounded more scary. We were not supposed to stay up late at night. But, after the coast was clear and the night nurse busied herself at the nurses' station, I turned up the volume of my radio to enable the other girls to share my prize possession. Some of our favorite programs were: "Baby Snooks,"

"Blondie," "Lux Presents Hollywood" and "The Lone Ranger." Sometimes, the nurse caught us, and after much pleading, if she was understanding, we were allowed to listen another half hour to complete the program.

There was an eerie silence in the room after the radio was turned off. I did not feel tired and I was not ready for sleep. That is when I thought of the past. After the war, I heard of some Jewish children whose parents had been killed in the concentration camps. The children had miraculously survived by being hidden in convents, and in the homes of heroic Christians. Now, they were orphans. I felt fortunate to have come out of this terror with both of my parents. My best friend Ruth, whom I met at Terezin, and so many other Jewish children were killed by the Nazis. I felt doubly guilty for having survived, and having my parents. I thought, *What is so special about me? Ruth was much smarter than I, and could have become a famous artist.* Sometimes, I imagined that I was an orphan and I tried to feel the pain that each child must be going through. This experience of sharing their pain freed me from any further feelings of guilt.

I had many nightmares, always the same bad dream. We were in Terezin and had our orders to go to the "East." Sometimes, only my parents were on the list, other times I was the one to be deported. I *always* woke up in a cold sweat. My parents suffered similarly. Once we spoke about our dreams.

I asked my mother to bring my doll, Marlene, to the hospital. She had been my constant companion since my second birthday. Now, I wanted her to share this new phase of my life. She sat on a hospital dresser next to my bed. I spent endless hours playing with her, speaking to her in

80

English, and hoping that she understood me. I tried out new words and phrases on her, and I looked at her blue eyes and smile for approval. Everyone else always corrected my English and made me feel uncomfortable. Because she never criticized or humiliated me, Marlene was the best listener.

Once in a while, one of us was wheeled in a wheelchair, or on a stretcher, to the "conference." I remember being taken on a stretcher to many such meetings. I was picked up by a special hospital aide and moved out of the ward into an elevator down to an underground area. Sunshine Cottage was connected by tunnels to the other medical facilities of Grasslands Hospital. We arrived in a waiting area, where I saw adult patients on stretchers and in wheelchairs. When my turn came I was rolled into a room full of doctors. It looked like a theatre because of the way they were seated. Dr. Childress stood in the front of the room. He introduced me as, "This is the one from one of those camps." Then my case was presented. I was told by my roommates that the conference was very important. It was the time when privileges and future medical procedures were decided. A bronchoscopy was ordered at one such conference, because my chest still sounded congested. This was extremely painful, performed in the operating room. All of the children dreaded it.

Privileges depended on one's state of health, and they were granted in a certain order. First, one was allowed to take a bath in the bathtub and walk to the bathroom. Then, fifteen, thirty minutes, and one hour out of bed. Ward privileges were the best. This meant that one could be out of bed most of the day, and even go outside of the hospital, except during daily rest period after lunch. We were supposed to sleep at this time, but few of us did. The last level of privileges came shortly before one was to be discharged from the hospital. It took me six months long to reach the first stage of privileges. After washing myself in bed for so long, my first "real bath" felt sensational. Many more months followed until I was allowed to leave my bed prison.

We had a playground furnished with swings and monkey bars. There was also a small empty lot, a short distance from the hospital. We used this space as a garden. One of the nurses encouraged us and showed us how to plant corn and other vegetables. Every day we looked for progress in their growth.

Grassland's main building had a large hall, where movies were sometimes shown to the patients and staff. It was a great treat for us to be allowed to attend these showings. Once in a while, a caravan of wheelchairs with happy children aboard snaked its way through the underground maze of tunnels to the film show. At least a year went by before I was granted the privilege of being picked up by the movie crew and pushed in a wheelchair to the event. One of the movies I saw was "Alexander's Ragtime Band." At such times, we girls fought to wear the best dresses provided by the hospital's laundry department. We wanted to make a good impression and pursuaded one of the student nurses to help us fix our hair. They made cork-screw curls by winding our hair around long pieces of gauze. The gauze was pulled out after a few hours, and we all looked like Shirley Temple.

◆ ◆ ◆

I remember seeing my first movie in Germany. It was in 1941, just before Jews were required to wear the yellow Star of David. Jews were forbidden to attend movie theatres. Papa decided that before we were branded with this ugly symbol, he would sneak us into a theatre in Stuttgart. I could hardly wait for school to be finished. I thought all day of our plan, and I had all kinds of ideas of how a movie would look. The ticket sales clerk did not look at us with suspicion. We entered the almost completely dark theatre. There was a large screen. It was as if a giant photograph came suddenly alive. A double feature children's program was shown: "Punch and Judy" came first; then a German fairy-tale. Luckily no one recognized us.

◆ ◆ ◆

There were never enough nurses to give us proper care. I helped to take care of the younger children when I was on advanced privileges. I gave them baths and washed their hair. It was during these last stages of privileges that I wrote the play, "Going Sled Riding," for an assignment from the hospital school held in our rooms.

At the end of 1947, during my second year at Sunshine Cottage, my parents pursuaded the doctors to let me spend a few days at home after Christmas. I was given instructions to follow the same routine as in the hospital. It was wonderful to enter the "real" world again. Once at home, we decided to break a few rules. I begged Papa to take me on a subway ride. We rode a short time on the train and came home. Snow began to fall in globs and it soon became apparent that we were in a blizzard. The radio reported that it was one of the worst snow falls in years. Because of the lack of transportation, I returned later to the hospital than my permission stated, with a sore throat, cough and fever. Some privileges were taken away. I was again at the bed rest stage.

There were very sad times on the ward, especially when some children were told that their mothers or fathers suffering from the same disease died in the adult medical facility of Grasslands. We had a few pairs of sisters to whom this happened. No child died on our ward during my two year stay. But, I was told that just before my arrival, a boy died from complications caused by the tuberculosis.

The student nurses rotated through the other medical facilities. One of them must have spoken to a Jewish woman patient in the main building about me. One day I received a little package from her which contained a small bottle of perfume and dusting powder, and was addressed to: "The little refugee girl on Ward 200." We became pen pals, but I never got to meet her. I do not recall her name.

Going Sled Riding

CHARACTERS

Harry

Inge

Miss Mahoney

Earl

Miss Kohn

Miss Cousins

Mary-Ann

Rose Mary

Vina

Robert

Angelina

(The children in Ward 200 are getting ready for school.)

Miss Mahoney: Earl, did you take your bath?

Earl: No, Harvey is taking his now.

Miss Mahoney: You take youts right after Harvey, understand?

Earl: Yes, Miss Mahoney.

(Earl finally is ready for school and so are the others.)

Inge: Miss Mahoney please part my hair?

Miss Mahoney: Is that all right Inge?

Inge: That's fine! Thank you very much.

Miss Cousins: Children are you all ready for school?

Group: Yes Miss Cousins.

(Finally Miss Kohn arrives)

Miss Kohn: O my how nice you look this morning, Rosemary, where did you get that pretty dress?

Rose-Mary: Mommy gave it to me.

Miss Kohn: That's fine Rose Mary.

Miss Kohn: Did you feed the birds yet children?

Group: Yes Miss Kohn we saw a red bird this morning what kind of bird is that?

Miss Kohn: That is a cardinal pretty isn't he?

Group: Yes.

Mary-Ann: May I go to school today Miss Kohn?

Miss Kohn: I don't think to-day but tomorrow.

Mary-Ann: Oh! Miss Kohn.

(The children go to the schoolroom and work quietly until recess.)

Miss Kohn: You may have recess now children.

Group: O goody, O goody, goody.

Going Sled Riding

Vina:	Miss Kohn may we *please* go outside to-day?
Miss Kohn:	I don't know. Ask Miss Cousins.
Vina:	Alright.
Vina:	Miss Cousins may we go out please.
Miss Cousins:	I will ask Miss Mahoney, did you finish your school so you can go outside at 10:15?
Vina:	Yes.
Miss Cousins:	Miss Mahoney will yuo take the kids out, huh?
Miss Mahoney:	Yes Miss Cousins.

(The time comes—10:15.)

Miss Kohn:	You may go now Vina, Inge, and Earl. Harvey will have to finish his reading first.
Harvey:	Miss Kohn I aint going to read only one more page.
Miss Kohn:	Listen Harvey when you are a teacher then you can tell the children what to do. OKay, but not now.
Harvey:	I guess so.

(Harvey is finished with his work.)

Harvey:	Good-bye Miss Kohn.
Miss Kohn:	Good-bye Harvey.

(He gets his sled and hurries to meet the other children on a hill.)

Inge:	Vina, Harvey is coming. Come on, let's go and meet him.
Vina:	O.K. let's hurry and go down with our sled.
Miss Mahoney:	Watch out children and be careful!
Inge:	Yes Miss Mahoney.
Vina:	Isn't it fun to go sled riding Inge.
Inge:	It sure is.
Vina:	Here we are.
Inge:	Oh Harvey, did you make out alright?
Harvey:	You betcha.
Harvey:	Let's put our sleds at one place and have a race.
Miss Mahoney:	No you may not because it is too dangerous.
Vina:	Too bad, too bad. Gee whiz, gee whiz.
Miss Mahoney:	I guess we have to go back now. Did you have a good time?

Going Sled Riding

Group:	Yes, Miss Mahoney.
Miss Mahoney:	When you come back to the ward before you come in take your rubbers off.

(When they have their coats off then they come into the ward.)

Inge:	Hey Angelina you know what?
Angelina:	What?
Inge:	Today we had a snowball fight, the girls against the boys and the girls won. Ha, ha.
Earl:	That isn't funny?
Angelina:	I'm glad you won.
Earl:	Yeah, of course girls would say that. Tomorrow we will beat them, Harvey won't we?
Harvey:	Sure.
Robert:	Of course.
Miss Cousins:	Now no fighting or nobody will go out tomorrow.
Earl:	Okay.
Harvey:	But the girls started the fight.
Miss Cousins:	Now Harvey be a gentleman won't you?
Harvey:	Be good and be a gentleman thats too much for me.
Miss Cousins:	Now Harvey behave yourself. Shame on you.
Miss Cousins:	Miss Mahoney were the kids good outside or did they give you any trouble?
Miss Mahoney:	No, but they wanted to race with their sleds and I didn't let them.
Miss Cousins:	Thats it, Miss Mahoney, you did the right thing.
Miss Mahoney:	I am glad you think so.

(Miss Mahoney and Miss Cousins hug each other and pat each other on the back.)

Inge:	Lets sing a song! Altogether, shall we?
Group:	Fine, what shall we sing?
Inge:	I think I'm laughing would be a good one.
Group:	Good lets go.

(The song ends with laughter.)

Group:	Ha, Ha, Ha, that was fine.

(And all are happy again.)

Miss Smyth (student nurse).
On back of photograph:

11/19/46

To Inga,

A very sweet kid—my case study—May your life be very sweet and pleasant from now on.

Always keep that smil on your face.

Best of luck

Always –

Anna M. Smyth
Grasslands Student
Sunshine Cottage

Last row: Miss Ouisely, Harry and Inge. Front row: Frankie, Kathy and Harvey.

July 5, 1947

Dearest Inge:

Trouble is only opportunity in Work Clothes. to take youns as stepping stones to gain your gold

Anne Quisley.

CHAPTER TWELVE

Sunshine Cottage Days

As time went on I got used to the hospital routine. Some days had special significance. Tuesday was Gastric Day. Each of us was subjected to this torture every other week. There were times when interns, doctors just out of medical school, were assigned to us. They were often inexperienced with the procedure, and I showed them how to do it, by pushing the tube down my nose by myself. There was always much excitement on this day. The children cried and were upset—some more than others. I remember that seven-year-old Mary-Ann always made the most fuss. This made such an impression on me that I wrote a play about her at that time, "Mary-Ann Gets A Gastric."

Wednesday was Volunteer Day and special for us. Our beds were pushed into one area of the ward. A group of ladies lead by Miss Besse came with a truckload of toys with which we were allowed to play for a few hours. Many times they brought along a piano, and we sang. Sometimes, they had bells and cymbals and we were encouraged to play them. The combination of piano and these sounds was like an orchestra.

While I was on complete bed rest for over a year, my activities were limited. I spent much time playing with paper dolls, dressing and undressing them, and weaving stories around them. Comic books and coloring books were very popular on Ward 200. We always fought over the books and who would get the best color assortment of crayons. Each child wanted first choice. *Superman* and *Batman* were our favorites. Sometimes jigsaw puzzles were donated by charitable organizations. We especially welcomed those with many pieces because they challenged us. Children who had out of bed privileges joined us. Our beds were pushed together to enable us to reach the pieces deposited on a table. We "worked" feverishly to complete the pictures. "Jacks" was a popular game. Small, metal jacks that looked like miniature jacks used to hoist cars were thrown on a table. You had to pick them up in a particular order, one at a time, then two, and so on. But, first you had to throw up a small ball, grab the jacks each time without touching another, and catch the ball before it bounced back on the table. Woe to the person who dropped the ball! There was not always someone around to pick it up and the game ended suddenly. On rare occasions, one of us sneaked out of bed to retrieve the ball.

One day we were daring and had a pillow fight. I fell out of bed and injured my head, and had to have X-rays taken. Nothing was broken, but I felt dizzy for quite some time.

Christmas was the best holiday for us. The volunteers brought a small Christmas tree, which we all helped to decorate. It was given to me as a special treat.

Hanukkah, the Jewish Festival of Lights, also celebrated in December, is close to Christmas. But, the Jewish calender depends on the phases of the moon, not a set number of days to a month as the Christian calendar does. So Hanukkah comes on different days every year. This holiday commemorates the victory of the Maccabees, a heroic group of Jewish fighters over the Syrian Greeks in 165 BC. Antiochus IV, the Seleucid King of Syria had tried to stop the observance of Judaism. The Hebrew word Hanukkah means "dedication." The temple in Jerusalem was cleansed and rededicated. This occasion is celebrated every year with the lighting of candles on a menorah, an eight-branched candlestick, and the singing of hymns, merrymaking, and the exchange of gifts. One candle is lit on the first day, every day an additional candle is lit until eight are burning on the last. This ritual reminds us of the miracle of the oil found in the temple that was to last one day, but burnt for eight. My parents brought me a Hanukkah menorah and candles. The decorated Christmas tree and Hanukkah menorah stood next to each other on my dresser. I hoped that God would not mind this order of things.

We all received many presents from different organizations and school children at Christmas time. Some of the children placed their names and a message inside the gift. I remember becoming pen pals with Mary Glowney this way.

All of us waited for the biggest event, a joint Christmas party with the polio ward downstairs. Wheelchairs and stretchers were loaded with jubilant children and moved downstairs to join the other group. There, the two wards were separated like soldiers of opposing armies. The highlight of the day was Santa's appearance with a present for each of us.

Mr. Wise, our porter became our confidant. This gentle Black man always had a smile and kind word for us. He picked up our dropped balls or paper dolls, and kept our rooms sparkling clean. We decided to form a secret club—"The Junior Justice Society," and made him the supervisor.

There were many dull days and we looked for any kind of excitement. A prison was near Grasslands Hospital. We sometimes saw the prisoners working on the grounds surrounding Sunshine Cottage, mowing the grass and caring for the flowers and shrubs. We spoke with them from our windows. They were really friendly, and we could not understand why they were in jail. I thought, *The prisoners are more free than us, we are the 'real' prisoners chained to our beds.*

Miss Kohn, our teacher came a few times each week, in the morning to conduct a variety of classes in our rooms. Most of the children were bed-bound. Since we were not supposed to have any strain, classes were not long. I welcomed this opportunity to improve my English. I received a mathematics assignment book, because that was one of my poorest subjects. We learned about how people lived in far away countries. I remember reading about China's rice paddies.

One day Miss Kohn let us do a science experiment. She said, "We'll place one flower pot with a blooming red flower into a closet in complete darkness, the other we'll keep in the sunlight on the window sill. Then in a few days, we'll see which one will look better." All of us waited with anticipation to see what the locked up flower would look like. Nothing was happening to the one near the window. To our surprise, when Miss Kohn took the plant out of the darkness, its petals had fallen off, and it looked sick. Miss Kohn's lesson was: "Flowers need sunlight to stay healthy." And so, my love for science was born.

Although, there was an official classroom, most of the children on our ward never got to use it, since we were on strict bed rest much of the time. Once, Miss Kohn gave us an assignment to write our life stories. These were displayed on the wall of the classroom and shown to our parents and other visitors on Sunday. We were wheeled on stretchers and wheelchairs to take part in this presentation. My account showed me still fearful of revealing my Jewish identity because I stated that a church instead of a synagogue was my place of worship.

At least eighteen months passed before I was allowed to stay out of bed a considerable amount of time. Then I joined the other children with similar privileges in our classroom and we learned about the conservation of plants and animals. Vina and I were asked to paint with water colors two pictures of a forest before and after a fire. Both of us were pleased with the result. Miss Kohn even took photographs of us standing next to our paintings.

Mary-Ann Gets a Gastric

CHARACTERS

1. Mary-Ann   2. Dr. Prout
3. Miss Ouisley   4. Earl
5. Vina   6. Nurse

Scene - Ward 200

Time - Night 7 P.M.

Our scene is in a ward. It is night time and the nurse went out a minute.

Earl: Who gets the gastric tomorrow, Vina?

Vina: I don't know, but I hope I don't get one.

Earl: If I go in the office and see will you tell on me?

Vina: No, not unless I have to.

(Earl goes into the office and sees some names and gets excited.)

Earl: Vina, Mary-Ann gets a gastric.

Vina: Who else?

Earl: Bobby and Sandra.

(Meanwhile Miss Ouisley comes into the ward and sees Earl in the office.)

Miss Ouisely: What are you doing in the office, Earl?

Earl: O my, I was just looking who was going to get a gastric.

Miss Ouisely: Bad boy!

(As night falls every body is in bed sleeping. Tuesday morning is an exciting day. The day nurses are coming in.)

Mary-Ann: Nurse, am I going to get a gastric?

Nurse: Let me see, O yes, you are and don't you start crying.

(The Doctor comes in, Mary-Ann starts crying. The Doctor starts with Mary-Ann.)

Dr. Prout: Now listen, Mary-Ann, will you stop fooling and swallow this rubber tube?

(Crying, Mary-Ann starts to swallow the tube.)

Mary-Ann: When is it going to be over?

(Now it's over).

Dr. Prout: Now, was that so bad?

Mary-Ann: Yes! I mean no!

I

My Life.

I was born in kippenheim
i.b. in Germany on Dec. 31. 1934. My father was
born in the same place, but my mother was born
in Jebenhausen in Germany. I stayed for a long time
there but sometimes I went to my Grandma's house.
When I was born my fathers parents and one of his
brothers where dead. My mother's parents where still
living.

Well it happened one November
day on a Saturday my Grandpa was in the church and
my father went too, but some of the Nazis took my father
and Grandpa to Dachau in a Concentrationcamp. I
was about 4 years that time and after they took my
father and Grandpa some of the Nazi boys came and
threw stone blocks into our windows and broke
everything they could. I was standing in the hall and
a big block of stone came right to me but my mother
pulled me away so it couldn't hit me. When I was
6 years old I went to the school but was not allowed
to go in the school in our city because I was a
different religion and I had to go 45 minutes with

II

the train to go to school. When I was in the city
the children called me bad names because I had a
different religion. In 1942 they took me and my family
to a concentration camp and then they took everything we
had except the clothes we had on and we had to wear a
big star with "Jew" written on every cloth we had.
From our camp they took transports to go to Aushwitz
into the gas chamber and we were a lot of times in
the transport ready to go but we came out of it again.
One day it happened they told the whole camp to go
on a big plain and all around stood S.S. men pointing
their guns at us. We were there mostly the hole day
standing up. That was in November and it was very
cold. It was very dark and they changed their minds
about killing us and we had to go back to the camp.

Two years after the war was over
the S.S. men tried to kill us, It happened like this
I was standing on the street and I saw many cars and
tanks go by and I thought to myself I hope that
nothing happens but when I finished thinking I heard
a big noise and I ran as fast as I could to my
parents. My mother was thinking I was dead, but my

97

III

father said it was a hand grenade that the Nazis
threw in and my father said a grenade can not go easily
through three or four houses, so we went to the third
house hole in the earth. All I took with me was a
prayer book for to pray to the Lord for help. One
man got killed because the grenade went right into
the room where he was. The Nazis tried to shoot the
whole camp but it was too late because the Russians
were too near by. So at ten minutes to nine the
Russians came I couldn't belive it for happiness,
They freed us. But then most of the people had
typhus and the camp was on barrier, and so we
couldn't go home right away.

        About 6 weeks passed and our
city from home send a bus to get us so we came
home to Stuttgart there they fixed a house for the
people and the first good food in years. We had nuddle
soup. We stayed there about a week and a letter came
from my uncle from America. Then we wanted to get
our own house back. When we came the people fixed
a room for us and decorated it with flowers. My father
started a nice store again in Göppingen in our apartment.

Mostly every day Amerikan soldiers came to see us and brought me candy. A little while after I came to America on the boat Marin Perch I got sea sick but I didn't care. We lived with my uncle for a little while but then my parents started to work for people. I had a bad cold so my mother went with me to the doctor and the doctor said I had to go to the hospital right the next day. My sickness was T.B.C. that I caught in the camp. I am here now over fourteen month and the doctore said I am doing fine. My father and mother now live in Brooklyn. I have many friends here and we have school too.

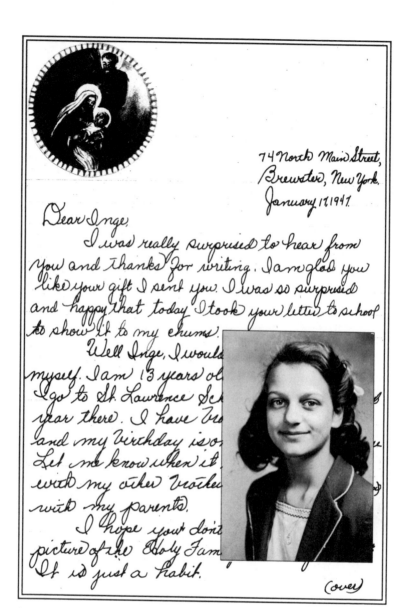

74 North Main Street,
Brewster, New York.
January 17, 1941.

Dear Inge,

I was really surprised to hear from you and thanks for writing. I am glad you like your gift I sent you. I was so surprised and happy that today I took your letter to school to show it to my chums.

Well Inge, I would myself. I am 13 years ol I go to St. Lawrence Sc year there. I have b and my birthday is o Let me know when it with my other broth with my parents.

I hope you don't picture of the Holy Fam It is just a habit.

(over)

Letter from my penpal, Mary Glowney (pictured).

100

All best wishes
to my friend Inge
from Eleanor Besse

Best Wishes from Eleanor Besse, Director of Volunteers.

Mr. Wise,
our porter.

MEMBERSHIP CARD OF
JUNIOR JUSTICE SOCIETY CLUB

This certifies that Inge
Auerbacher is a member of the
Junior Justice Society Club and must
abide by all rules.
   (signed by)   Inge Auerbacher, Pres.
Illinois Wise   Vina Grady
(Supervisor)   (Secretary)

Children from Ward 200.
Front: Rose-Mary
Second Row: Harvey, Frankie, Harry, Sandra
Back: Inge

CHAPTER THIRTEEN

God Hears Everywhere

I was the only Jewish child at Sunshine Cottage. Since meals often contained pork, a meat strictly forbidden to people of the Jewish faith, at first I left it uneaten on the plate. I told my parents about this problem. Mama said: "Eat everything now, and you'll get well faster. When you're at home, you can observe the dietary laws again." The first few bites of this strange meat almost made me sick, because I felt that I was doing something wrong. In time I got used to it.

We all looked forward to the day when the Sunday School Man, Chaplain Townsend, came. He was a friend to us all, whether Catholic, Protestant or Jewish. He distributed colorful booklets of bible stories that fascinated me. I wanted to learn more about the extraordinary man, Jesus, whom they called the Son of God.

Chaplain Townsend brought a rabbi to my bedside. The rabbi also gave me bible stories to read and I became well acquainted with the Old and New Testament. My religious training in Judaism had been limited to what I learned at home: I never had the possibility to attend official religious classes. In the concentration camp friends taught me some Hebrew songs. Papa gave me lessons in reading the prayers in Hebrew. And, I almost mastered identifying the strange words written in a different alphabet, and reading from right to left instead of the usual left to right.

There was no synagogue on the hospital grounds and my longing to hear a Sabbath and a Holiday service had to be satisfied by infrequent radio services for people unable to attend a synagogue. I was a rapt listener and sang the familiar Hebrew chants with the cantor.

I felt cheated when the other children got dressed up to go to church on Sunday. They pleaded with me to join them. Because I did not want to be different and to be left out, I decided I would. I had never been in a church and I did not know how one behaved. *Could anyone tell that I was Jewish?* I followed the others; folded my hands, knelt down, and listened to the prayers. My best friend in the camp, Ruth, was partially Jewish, but reared as a Christian. It seemed very peculiar to me for her to fold her hands when she prayed. I was never told to do that by my parents. Later, I asked them about this custom. "Jewish people don't do that, just continue to say your prayers without folding your hands. God will hear you," they replied. I thought back to the hospital church service. Although the hymns were strange, I felt good for a while and not out of place. No one pointed a finger at me saying, "This is not your church, you don't belong here!" Then guilt overcame me. I had my own religion and Hebrew was our language for prayer. *What was I doing here? God will punish me!* Finally I understood that God is all Good and would listen to me in any place of worship. Silently, I said the "Shema Israel," a very special Hebrew prayer, because God hears everywhere.

Doctor Medina, one of our women resident doctors liked me, more perhaps, because we were both immigrants. She came from Cuba. When one of the children prepared for her first Communion she asked me if I would like to prepare as well? "I'll buy you a beautiful white dress and you'll look just like a little bride," she said. This offer sounded very good, because being Christian seemed so much less troublesome than being Jewish. But my conscience won. Dr. Medina was disappointed, yet understanding of my feelings.

While helping the other children learn the Catechism, I too learned this education and the prayers, "Our Father" and "Rosaries."

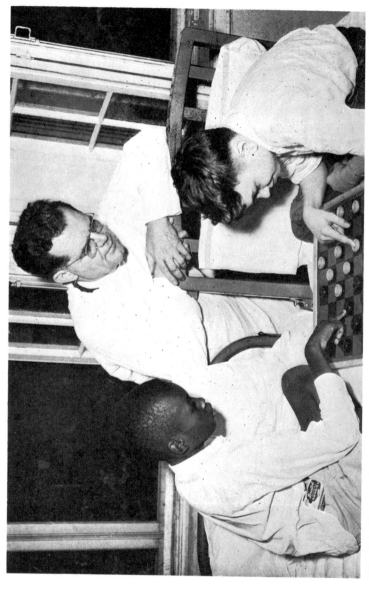

Chaplain Townsend with children of Ward 200.
Courtesy of the Archives of the Episcopal Church

The "Sunday School man" guides beginners in faith which they carry with them into world.

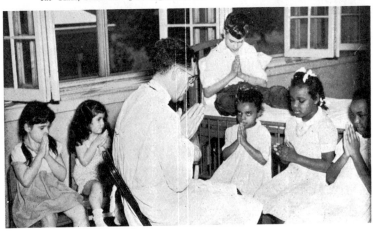

Sunday School.
Courtesy of the Archives of the Episcopal Church.

CHAPTER FOURTEEN

Love Conquers All

I woke up one morning thirteen—a teenager. The little girl became a young woman. I still liked playing with paper dolls and my doll, Marlene, but felt a little foolish enjoying these activities. Now that I was grown up, I was not supposed to hang on to the toys of childhood. But, where were the playtime years? They were too short. During the war years I was expected to act grown up. Finally, the time was right to be a child and do the things that children like. *Why was my life so mixed up?* I felt cheated again.

There was little change in our ward's population. It seemed no one ever went home. Harvey, six, and Rose Mary, two, were there all of their short lives. A new admission to the ward was always cause for excitement. We had many questions. Who was the new patient? A boy or girl? How old? Usually a student nurse filled us in on some of the details. One day a new patient was a fifteen year old Puerto Rican boy. However, many months passed until I got to see him.

One day Harry was wheeled to my bedside to help me with a difficult jigsaw puzzle. We soon became close friends and discovered we had much in common. We were given ward privileges at the same time, and since both of us still had problems with English, we were given the same class assignments by our teacher. One of these was to draw a picture of our "memories" of home. Harry was a good artist and drew many exotic scenes showing swaying palm

108

trees on an island surrounded by an aqua ocean. *Puerto Rico must be a beautiful place.* I learned a great deal about this different place. In Germany there were no palm trees or blue oceans. Harry's pictures introduced me to a different culture and way of life. I was surprised by how much shorter he was than I.

Ten year old Frankie was in the bed next to Harry's in the large room of the wards, "Boys End." His mother brought him on a Sunday visit a so-called "atomic bomb ring" which she received for mailing a cereal box top and twenty five cents to a food company. It was supposed to look like shooting sparks when viewed in darkness. Night had not yet come, so we built a tent-like structure with pillows and blankets on one of the beds. All three of us crawled into our "tent." Frankie was first to look into the ring and seemed excited with what he saw. In the meantime, I felt something moist touch my hand and I screamed, "Harry, don't kiss me!" Now, I knew Harry liked me not only as a friend, but also in a grown up way. Then Harry and I got a chance to look inside the ring.

Next day, we made another tent, but this time we did not invite Frankie to join us. Harry held the ring close to my eyes. His arms were soon around me. He held me close to him and I melted in his arms. The wonderful feeling of a first kiss on the lips followed. The ring's sparks, Harry's kiss and hug made me feel like I was floating on a cloud. He whispered into my ear, "You are a beautiful girl, Inge, and you have beautiful blue eyes." *My eyes are brown.* "I will always keep a picture of you." These episodes continued for a short while, until we both got tired of setting up a tent.

One night Harry sneaked into to the "Girls End" and brought me a Cupie doll, a doll with wings symbolizing love. We set up a walky-talky system using paper cups connected by a long string, thinking that the others could not hear our conversations. This method never worked well, but I did hear him say, "Inge, I love you very much do you love me?" The doctors became concerned about our relationship and our "growing up." Dr. Medina started to explain to me what responsibilities being a woman had, but she seemed too embarrassed to finish the lesson. She did recommend that I no longer walk around in my pajamas without wearing a robe over them, for that was the proper way a young lady should appear before men.

The "facts of life" were almost a total mystery to me. I had been told as a small child that when one placed a cube of sugar on the window sill, a stork would pick it up and bring a baby brother or sister. I followed this advice many times, but I never received my reward of a baby brother. Mama was too embarrassed to speak to me. One resident doctor asked me a few questions about what I knew, after I had my first period. But, he lost his courage to fully explain everything in words that I could understand.

Ruth and I saw pregnant women in the concentration camp. We wondered about their huge bellies. *Were they sick? How did they become that way?* Ruth got up her nerve and asked her parents about these grotesque-looking women. They did not give her an explanation, but punished her for asking such awful questions. I was too afraid to question my parents. Ruth and I could not understand why her questions aroused hostility. We reasoned there was an evil associated with this "huge belly" condition to foster such an angry response. Our curiosity drove us to timidly ask an older girl, Margot, what she knew about it. "They have a baby in their belly, you silly girls. When a married man and woman love each other, they can have a baby," she said. Ruth and I thought if it was that easy, why couldn't we have babies? We were getting bored with our dolls. They did not respond to us when we embraced them. They did not feel warm and never cried. There was something missing in them. Margot made baby getting sound so easy. We decided to get husbands.

Most men, women, and children were forced to live in separate quarters in the camp. Because, our fathers were disabled war veterans from World War I, we were permitted to live as a family in a designated area. This on-site special treatment did not protect us from being shipped to the gas chambers at Auschwitz. Margot, her younger sister Gerda, and her parents also lived in our disabled war veterans quarters. Ruth and I were not satisfied with Margot's answer and turned to Gerda for more information. We confided in her and she volunteered to help us find husbands. The three of us went to the children's home and eyed a few boys playing in the fenced-off yard. Peter was chosen for me, and another boy for Ruth. I never spoke one word to my "husband-to-be."

Ruth and I shared bunk beds. I slept on the upper level, and she on the lower. We promised not to tell anyone of our secret plan. We whispered to each other every night of our impending motherhood. We carefully packed our doll's clothing in a torn sheet, and saved small amounts of sugar from our meager food rations in a little sack. These items would serve as clothing and food for the baby. We had heard rumors that one must have permission from the camp authorities to give birth to a child. How would we get these papers, especially when no one was supposed to know of our impending motherhood?

Ruth and I looked at our bellies often, but they did not begin to swell. The opposite was happening. We became thinner each day, because of the poor nutrition. As time went on, we became disillusioned. *Did I miss doing something?* Our plans were suddenly ended. In late September, 1944, Ruth and her parents were sent to the East. After Ruth's departure, I turned my attention again to my doll, Marlene. She now gave me comfort and felt more cuddly than before.

Harry was given a new experimental drug not yet used in cases like mine. He made a miraculous recovery and was soon sent home. I was sad and missed him very much. At night I looked out the window and thought back to the time when we two went to the hospital movies. He would hold my hand. I wore my best dress from home and a rose in my hair to make him feel proud of me. At Christmas, he sent a card from home, and I was overjoyed that he had not forgotten me.

A hospital call-board with flashing numbers on our ward was used as a paging system for the doctors. We tried to figure out who was being called. Vina and I thought up a game to let numbers represent letters. For example: A equals 1, B equals 2, and so on. The letter H was 8. One day, 3, 5, 8 were lit, and the combination of 3 plus 5 equals 8; spelling out the letter H. As the numbers flashed on the board, the doors to our ward opened and Harry walked in. He came to visit us. This was the last time I saw him.

Harry and I were not the only "love birds" on our ward. We sometimes saw Miss Cousins, our head nurse, and Dr. Nice, a resident doctor, sneak a kiss outside of the swinging doors. All of us watched this couple closely for any unusual signs. We wondered if they would get married.

◆ ◆ ◆

I became restless as time wore on. Days became weeks and months. I wanted to escape from this "new prison." My parents decided to leave the Streim Residence after one year. The Streims felt bad about this news. They liked my parents and hated to see them leave. They even gave them a set of dishes as a farewell gift. Papa luckily had found a low-rent apartment in the Bushwick section of Brooklyn. They moved into our new home in the fall of 1947. An elderly Austrian lady from the residence liked Mama so much, she begged my parents to take her along to our apartment to live with us.

Although I was not completely well, my parents pursuaded the doctors to let me go home in the summer of 1948. I had spent two years at Sunshine Cottage. Mama was able to take care of me at home now. Papa's retail business selling plastic products worked out so well that he expanded it to include linens and other textiles. Our life was becoming better and my parents seemed happy with their improved status.

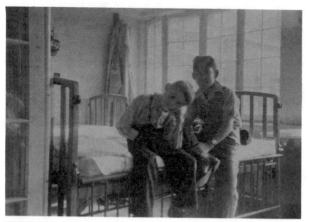

Harry on right, Franklie on left.

Earl and Harry.

CHAPTER FIFTEEN

Brooklyn Is My Home

In the summer of 1948 I could hardly believe that I was finally released from Ward 200. My prison term was over. I felt a peculiar sensation in my stomach as I said good-bye to my "fellow inmates," doctors and nurses. I was sorry for my friends who had to remain and who I would, most likely, never see again. *Now, I can be a 'normal' person, and take part in previously forbidden activities. I will have no more gastric tests, silly rules and regulations to follow.*

Mama and a male friend of my parents picked me up by car. A soft breeze came through the open window. The car radio was on and Nat King Cole was singing "Nature Boy." This haunting melody had a strange effect on me. I was excited, happy, anxious and a little sad all at the same time...I had made so many friends in the hospital. *Who would become my new friends? Would they be nice to me? Would they ask questions about my past, and where I had been? Surely, I would keep my hospitalization a secret. That was no one's business. The nature of my illness would remain a mystery.* My parents had warned me in the hospital that when I got out I was never to tell anyone about my sickness, "Just tell them you were weak from the camp, and that you needed to build up your strength," they said. They knew that people were afraid to be near someone with a history of tuberculosis, and they wanted to protect me from being treated like an untouchable. They wanted to spare me the rejection that would surely follow me, if someone found out about my condition. Parents would tell their children, "Don't go near that girl, you might get sick from her!" Since I was no longer in the contagious state, and posed no danger to others, I was annoyed. *Why must I always hide something about my life? First, it was because I am Jewish, and now this?*

Mama sat beside me. I wore the new dress that she had brought me. She sensed that something was troubling me, and placed her arm on my shoulders: "Don't you like the new dress I bought for you? You look so beautiful in it. It's so nice to see you out of those pajamas. Things will be different from now on, you'll see." I smiled at her. Her words were so soothing.

Mama and I sat in the back seat. Our driver hardly spoke to us during the ride. I welcomed his silence. The last thing I wanted was to engage in small-talk. I watched the changing scenery, and marvelled at the kaleidoscope of images shooting past my window. Everything became a blur. It was like seeing a movie in fast forward. The scenery was constantly changing. Most everything in the hospital stayed the same. All was routine: rows of beds, white sheets, nurses, doctors, and crying children. This was such a different world, one that I had been part of before. A world that I had to get used to again.

After a two hour ride, we arrived at our new home on Chauncey Street, between Hopkinson and Saratoga Avenue, in Brooklyn. The block was a long row of attached brownstone houses, they all looked alike. We entered one of them and walked up to the third floor. There was no elevator. Papa was waiting for us. As he opened the door to our apartment, the familiar aroma of home-cooking welcomed me. The air was heavily scented with the pungent smell of sauerkraut, one of my favorite dishes. What a change from the medicinal odors of the hospital. Papa looked so strong and handsome without the white gown visitors were required to wear over their clothes in the hospital. He greeted me with a big hug and I knew that finally, we'd be a family again!

Mama introduced me to the elderly lady boarder who formerly lived at the Streim Residence for Senior Citizens. I was told to address her as "Omi," or granny in German. I noticed that Omi showed no interest in me. She mumbled to herself; oblivious to what was going on around her. Mama noticed my puzzled look and said, "Omi is living in her own world, try to be kind to her. Her condition comes with old age. Don't be afraid of her. She will not harm you."

Mama told me I could get up whenever I wanted. It was a special treat to sleep longer that first morning, and not be awakened by the loud hospital noises. The doctor had given my mother directions to follow certain rules, for although I was released from the hospital I was not completely well. I still needed much rest, and my temperature had to be taken both in the morning and at night.

The house was owned by the Auers, an Austrian couple, who lived in the apartment below ours. Mama explained that I must introduce myself and be very polite. So, the next day, I grabbed my mother's hand, and we both went downstairs to meet them. We spoke German with each other. Mrs. Auer said that I looked like a nice girl, and she hoped that I would not make too much noise to disturb her sick husband. She worked as a supervisor in a factory. Mr. Auer spoke with a soft voice and looked frail. He was almost blind and seemed a great deal older than his wife. Mrs. Auer was much shorter than her husband, and looked stern. I was uneasy in her presence.

Our apartment was called a "cold water railroad flat," because all the rooms were attached to each other in a straight line, and there was no central heating system. It was heated by kerosene stoves. The smell of the kerosene was terrible and made my eyes tear. I hated winter because of it. The bathroom had no heater, and it was very cold in the winter. Omi had her own room next to the kitchen. I was given a convertible couch to sleep on in the living room.

Papa's English was still poor, and he looked for German-speaking customers. He was told that many Germans settled in the Ridgewood section of Brooklyn, and in a few cities of New Jersey. Ridgewood did not produce enough customers, so he expanded his sales territory to New Jersey. Mama often helped him carry the heavy packages of sold merchandise to the subway very early in the morning. On some days he only carried his suitcase filled with samples of sheets, pillow cases, socks, underwear for men and women, towels and plastic goods and took the orders for them. Most of his customers bought on credit, and he had to collect money from them every week. He always came home from New Jersey very late and tired from these weekday selling trips.

No work was performed on Saturday, our Sabbath and day of rest. Papa always took a long nap in the afternoon while Mama and I went for a long walk. If Papa had a good week of sales, to celebrate our good fortune, Mama would buy a cake on Friday from what we affectionately called the "Blue Bakery," because of its blue awning. We ate this delicacy on Saturday afternoon. I always looked forward to this special treat.

Every Saturday night my parents sat in the kitchen with piles of notebooks spread on the table doing the tedious task of book-keeping. I had to be very quiet and undisturbing.

Every Sunday Papa and Mama went to the "Lower Eastside" of Manhattan to buy the customer ordered merchandise. Their destination was Delancey Street and the surrounding streets lined with wholesale stores owned by Jewish shopkeepers. The Lower Eastside was settled mainly by Jewish immigrants from Eastern Europe at the turn of the century. Many of them were poor. They found a safe haven in America, far from the deadly pogroms and anti-Semitic riots of Russia and Poland. They brought with them the customs of these countries and their Jewish traditions. A visit to the Lower Eastside included a feast of spicy aromas; the smell of pickled herring floating in a salty brine, and barrels of dilled pickles heavily laced with garlic. Street vendors sold hot "knishes," or potato cakes, and salty pretzels in winter, and ice cream in the summer. They pushed their loaded carts through the colorful streets and shouted out their wares. A variety of household items and clothing hung from clothes lines strung across the outside of the stores. Often, it was difficult to walk through the crowd of people and past the boxes filled with goods lining the store fronts. These narrow stores were housed in old houses in which merchandise nearly touched the ceiling. They were crammed full each Sunday with peddlers like Papa, haggling over prices. Loud voices in Yiddish and heavy accented English were heard everywhere.

Papa was known on the Lower Eastside as a tough bargainer. Tempers often flared, but shopowner and buyer were not bothered by this weekly ritual. They often shook hands and embraced each other after they compromised on a price for the goods. I always got a headache from all the screaming.

The best part of these shopping trips was our visit to one of the kosher restaurants, where we ordered bean soup. It was the cheapest item on the menu. Large bowls were filled to the brim with the thick, dark green soup. On each table sat a basket loaded with different varieties of bread. I liked the dark Russian bread with the crisp crust the best and spread it with a huge amount of butter. The combination of the delicious soup and bread filled me up for hours. A trip to the Lower Eastside was a special event.

When I began to miss my friends from the hospital, an older girl from the next house advised my mother to send me to the neighborhood candy store. "That's where everybody hangs out," she said. I felt shy and scared to go there, but after some encouragement from Mama I decided to give it a try. She walked me to the shop's door and quickly left before anyone saw us together. I felt peculiar entering this store containing strange looking things. *What, if no one speaks to me? I'd rather go back home.* I sat down at one of the back tables and ordered a coke. The place was empty, except for the owner and an occasional customer. I waited almost an hour, but no young people came. I went home feeling very disappointed. This was an "excursion" that I never repeated. I realized that I had to be my own best friend, and once again I reached out to my doll, Marlene, for companionship. By this time I had grown so close to her that I treated her as a part of me.

Realizing my loneliness, my parents surprised me with two goldfish swimming in a small glass bowl. I was overjoyed. The fish seemed always hungry and I fed them often. I talked to them and encouraged them to eat everything. One morning, one of my pets floated motionless belly-up on top of the water. The other goldfish soon followed. Perhaps he missed his partner and died from loneliness, or I over-fed him. I cried bitterly for days over the loss.

I spent many hours daydreaming of someday becoming a famous movie star or writer. In games of make-believe I could be and do anything my heart desired. Once, I pursuaded my mother to photograph me in a model-like pose holding an umbrella. The picture came out so well, that I really looked like one of the models in the magazines. *One day I will be famous and everyone will want to be my friend.* These lonely days continued for quite some time...the summer of 1948 seemed never to end. I desperately wanted to go to school, where I could meet people my age, but my wish was not granted. After receiving information from my doctor, the Department of Health decided that I was not well enough to enter public school. Therefore, The Board of Education enrolled me in a course of study for the homebound. They sent a teacher a few times a week to our home. Unfortunately, the teacher's visits did not last long. She was an elderly lady, who found it difficult to climb the three flights of stairs, and she soon resigned. I was left again to my daydreams.

Omi's daughter, Gretel, was a piano teacher, trained at a Conservatory of Music in Vienna. She offered to give me free lessons because she felt sorry for me. "You will see how music will make you happy, and you won't feel lonely anymore," she said.

My parents, hearing of a warehouse that sold used pianos, were able to purchase a huge Sohmer for fifty dollars. I felt a little guilty that Papa should spend a whole week's profit from his sales for it. Two delivery men groaned under its weight as they hoisted it up to our third floor apartment. Mrs. Auer checked the stairs. Thankfully, she was satisfied that no damage was made by the movers. I was afraid that something would go wrong, and Papa yelled at me, "You and your crazy piano! Now, we'll have to spend even more money for repairs." I breathed a sigh of relief when the delivery was successfully completed.

Lessons began and I became completely absorbed in the music, practicing at least four hours every day, until our next-door neighbors could not bear it anymore and threw shoes at the wall. Mr. and Mrs. Hicks had been so nice to us. I thought that they liked me. They had invited Mama and me to watch the Christmas Mass at St. Patrick's Cathedral on their new television set. Their rude behavior disappointed me, but I was not discouraged. Mama pleaded with them to endure me, and to let me continue my piano lessons. Gretel thought I was a gifted student, and should think of a future in music. I was happy that Mr. Auer had no complaints. He enjoyed the music and often complimented me, "You are getting better, you make fewer mistakes."

In the meantime, a new homebound teacher. Mrs. Smith, was assigned to me. We immediately became friends. She made sure that her lessons were stimulating and informative, and assigned long homework from text books that I had to pick up at the Board of Education. I welcomed this challenge and worked very hard at mastering my lessons. After a while, it was no longer fun studying alone. I wanted to ask many questions, but there was no one around to answer them. Papa was always away on his selling trips, and Mama was busy taking care of Omi and the household. I had little supervision with my studies. I could stop reading or writing whenever I felt like it. Often, I looked out of the window and watched children going and coming from school. How, I envied them! Then I thought, *Maybe, they would be jealous of me, not to be forced to attend school each day, and be burdened with tests and homework on a regular basis.* I felt better after I had a conversation with myself.

Papa sometimes attended services in the nearby synagogue. He met another father one Sabbath morning. They exchanged information about their "little" girls. Louise was brought to visit me that same day by her father. We looked at each other and laughed. Neither of us was little. We were tall for our age and wore adult, size ten shoes. She was also an only child, a year and a half younger than I. Both of us had dark, curly hair. I was happy that I finally met someone my own age. Louise and I promised to become friends for life. We shared our love for writing and read our poems to each other. Once we wrote about a fairyland together. Louise introduced me to the Public Library, and helped me get a library card. We sometimes went to the library together and took out piles of books; complaining all the way home over their weight. On one occasion, we bought a booklet of matches that were supposed to turn into small snakes when lit. We were afraid to light them but Louise gave it a try. When a small grey-green worm came out of the flame, we were disappointed with the outcome. We wondered if that was all that would happen. We decided that our money would have been better spent on ice cream.

Louise had many other friends from school, and was busy with school work and her Girl Scout group. I still felt isolated, because of my homebound classes. I wanted to join her Girl Scout group and was very disappointed when her mother said that it was filled. I did not see Louise very often.

I frequently went to our neighborhood Woolworth discount store to try on earrings and daydream. *Some day I will have enough money and buy all of them. Some day I will buy beautiful clothes and be an important person.*

I had many fears before I came home from the hospital. Would my parents treat me like an invalid? Was Papa still so strict? Some of my fears came true. Mama became very overprotective, "You must not strain yourself. Take a nap every day after lunch. Dress warmly. Be careful, don't catch a cold." It seemed like an endless chain of commands. Sometimes, I rebelled. It was almost like being in the hospital again. Mama would look hurt, "I only want to keep you well. I mean the best for you," she would say. Since he came home late at night, I did not see much of Papa. He was so tired by then, that he was left with little energy to criticize my behavior.

Sometimes, I used my sickness as an excuse to get my own way. Mama gave in to my whims, at times. On one of these occasions, I asked her if we could go to a dentist to straighten a protruding front tooth. I was told at the hospital, "Ask your parents to have that fixed." That front tooth really bothered me. I sometimes did not want to smile. It became very noticeable in photographs. Mama decided to take me to a specialist. The doctor pronounced his verdict. "Yes, it can be done. She will have to wear a brace for a few years. Can you pay the thousand dollars it will cost? The fifteen dollars for the visit would go toward the payment of the bill," he said. We decided not to give him an immediate answer, but to go home and think it over.

Feelings of guilt overcame me when we left the doctor's office. *How dare I ask my parents to make such a sacrifice! This was not a life or death situation. I could live with a crooked tooth. I'd try to be careful not to open my mouth so wide, and tilt my head at an angle for a photograph which would minimize the effect.* I begged my mother not to go on with the project. "You both work so hard for the money, and this is really an unnecessary thing. Let's save our money for a house," I said. It was many years later as an adult that I had my teeth straightened, and paid with my own, earned money.

Brooklyn is an experience. Jokes are made about it, but anyone who has lived here has a warm feeling for it. Brooklyn is where my life in America really began. Our kitchen window faced the backyard, where I saw a jungle of clotheslines criss-cross high above the backyards to large wooden poles. They looked like exposed veins, and were a housewife's lifeline. They seemed strained carrying their heavy load of assorted laundry. Once in a while when the lines froze, there was the winter disaster of a broken line. Mama considered this a major catastrophe, "Who would venture to climb up the tall pole and attach a new clothesline?"

There was a fire escape outside one of the kitchen windows. Fire escapes served as the poor man's terraces in this Irish-Italian, working-class neighborhood. Although it was illegal to keep anything on them, many people lined them with flower pots. Brooklyn summers were hot. There was no relief from the heat in the humid apartments. Men wearing tee shirts and shorts and women wearing sun dresses sat on the fire escapes. My parents warned me never to do this. "God forbid, you could fall to the yard!" No one owned an air conditioner. Our small fan only blew the heat around. To get out of the hot and humid air, we went to the air conditioned Colonial Movie Theatre near the Brooklyn Broadway. There was always a double feature. Sometimes, to take advantage of the delicious cool air, we stayed to see one film twice. I remember seeing two wonderful movies about India, "Sabu" and "Three Feathers." On designated evenings, to entice people to come to the movies, dinner plates and glasses were given to patrons.

Summertime evenings found people in lively conversations on the front stoops of the brownstone houses. This was also the time for "block parties," when one block was closed to traffic, tables loaded with homemade delicacies and lemonade lined the street, and colorful lights were strung between lamp posts. There was a carnival atmosphere as night fell. Music filled the air, and the street became a crowded dance floor.

A Brooklyn summer also meant an invasion by thousands of cockroaches. They crawled over everything, and were particularly visible when the lights were turned on at night. We stepped on them and crushed them with our hands. Only a gas, poisonous to roaches, helped control them. We placed the gas bomb in the kitchen, closed all the doors and windows, and left the apartment. We returned after a few hours and opened the windows to get rid of the gas. The kitchen floor was covered with a black carpet of dead roaches. We used a broom and shovel to get rid of them. Unfortunately, our "roach free" environment was short-lived. The process had to be repeated often.

Omi's health deteriorated, and she had to be placed in a nursing home. Mama was no longer tied to the house. Both of us decided that we could help out financially by selling aprons to people in the neighborhood. We knocked on many apartment doors. The "two ladies with the nice aprons" became part of the Chauncey Street scene. Many paid in fifty cents installments each week.

Just as everything fell into place, I became very sick again. My cough returned, much more severe than before, and I began to hemorrhage. Maybe, climbing all those stairs during our selling trips was harmful. I became very weak. *Is this the way you feel when you die?* I did not have enough strength to walk and had to be carried by my father to our car for my doctor's appointment in Scarsdale. Papa's health was not good either. He had developed a heart condition, and could not carry the heavy packages of merchandise anymore. He therefore bought a very old used car, which often did not run. On the day of my appointment with the doctor, it was badly damaged by a hit-and-run driver. Papa had to tie a rope around it to keep the doors on the right side closed.

The doctor examined me. My health had worsened and long rides would be too taxing. He told us to find a specialist closer to our home.

This turned out to be a lucky change. The new doctor immediately ordered the same drug for me as Harry had received at Sunshine Cottage. The drug, however, had a serious possible side effect. It could cause deafness. Mama was taught to inject me with the drug twice a day. She felt more emotional pain giving these needles than I did getting them. So, we found a nurse to continue my injections. Months passed and the new drug worked miracles. I felt strong enough to resume my school work.

Mrs. Smith had other home-bound students. As her means to get us to know each other, we were all going to create a magazine. We were to write about incidents from our pasts that would interest each other. I wrote about my first job baby-sitting in the concentration camp. I was nine years old and received potatoes as payment.

It was 1950 and I was fifteen years old. Louise was attending Hunter High School for gifted girls in Manhattan. Mrs. Smith told me her other homebound student, Jeanette, and I were to graduate from eighth grade. We were to join the graduation ceremony for "regular" students held at Abraham Lincoln High School in Brooklyn. Mama bought me a beautiful white dress and a corsage of red roses. But Jeanette and I were not allowed to join the other students in the procession to receive diplomas. We had to remain in our seats and were given our "special" certificates separately. Again, I was heartbroken to be left out.

Later, during her last visit, Mrs. Smith spoke to me about saving the memory of my graduation. "You should ask your parents to have a professional picture taken of you wearing your graduation dress." When I confronted my parents with her suggestion, Papa replied, "You have enough pictures of

yourself. We don't have money to waste for foolish things."
Mama did not give her opinion. The dam suddenly burst.
The frustrations and disappointments of my past
overwhelmed me. Full of rage, I threw myself on the floor,
crying hysterically, while pounding my fists on the linoleum.
"Why can't I ever be like other children? Everyone is having
their picture taken. Why do I always have to be left out?"
My parents stood over me, looking startled and scared. They
had never seen me act like this. But, Mama always had a
way to smooth out confrontations. She was known in our
family as a peacemaker. Speaking in a soft voice, Mama
tried to console me. "Please, my child, don't do this to us.
We understand your pain. We'll go to a photographer, and
you'll get your picture like the others." Papa remained
silent, no doubt thinking it best to let Mama handle the
situation. My mother's words worked wonders on me. I got
up off the floor and kissed both of my parents. I was
ashamed, and apologized for having thrown a temper
tantrum.

A few days after graduation, we took the corsage out of
the refrigerator where it had been stored to keep it alive and
we went to a photo studio. I was determined to look like a
'real' graduate in the picture.

Before Mrs. Smith and I finally parted she wrote in my
album, "Hitch your wagon to a star." I was ready for the
future and vowed to become the best student at Bushwick
High School in Brooklyn.

At Home in Brooklyn
in front of 485 Chauncey Street

Inge and parents.

Mama and Inge.

Inge at her piano.

6 / 30 / '50

To Inge:
Hitch your wagon to
a star!
M. M. Smith

From my Hombound Teacher. In my album.

Fourth of July—1776

Many, many years ago our fathers signed a Declaration,
It declared that America must have liberty, to be a free nation.
They rode on their horses to Philadelphia and answered the call,
To sign their names to the Declaration in Independence Hall.
It took away from them the everlasting fear,
To have England make their laws and to obey them clear.
For celebration the Liberty Bell was rung,
And all over the country, thankful songs were sung.
This was on the Fourth of July 1776, a great event in History,
For our fathers declared this country shall have Freedom
and Liberty.

Poem by Inge, 1950. From Daily Times, Homebound Magazine.

My First Earning

A couple of days ago, I was asked how I earned my first money. I really did not get any money for my work, but an important product as you will see later in the story.

It was like this: I was in a Concentration Camp in Europe at that time. Nobody was allowed to have any money there, the main thing was to get food—to still one's hunger. As you can now understand, I chose a product—food.

It happened like this: I was walking down a street on a cool Autumn day, when a lady suddenly spoke to me, and asked me if I could watch her little boy, Benny. He was in the carriage at the time. I said, "I will," then she asked me what I wanted for baby sitting. I told her I wanted some potatoes and she agreed. So I baby sat for her a few days a week. I was very proud of this because I could bring home some precious potatoes which are so wonderful to eat.

So now, dear reader, you can see it was just as exciting to earn those delicious potatoes as it would have been to earn money.

Written by Inge, 1950. From Daily Times, Homebound Magazine.

Miss "Sweet Sixteen" of 1950.

Graduation from Junior High School, Homebound classes, 1950.

CHAPTER SIXTEEN

Picking Up The Pieces

Finally, in the fall of 1950, I was permitted to be a "normal" teenager and began my "real" school career. In Germany I had not even completed first grade before I was sent to the concentration camp. After liberation I had nine months of schooling followed by the so-called classes of the hospital and homebound. I cried tears of joy and slept poorly the night before my first day of school at Bushwick High School in Brooklyn. I was as excited as on the night before I started first grade. Mama had bought me some new skirts and blouses and I had chosen my favorite new outfit, a green corduroy skirt, white long sleeve blouse, and red corduroy vest for the first day of high school. But I had unsettling thoughts. *Would I be able to do all of the school work requested of me? The other students must know much more than I. They will probably make fun of my lack of knowledge. Will the other students like me?* After these thoughts, most of my enthusiasm disappeared.

Suddenly, it was morning and sunlight streamed into my room. My heart started to beat quickly and I felt a combination of fear and joy. I dressed in a hurry, and joined my parents in the kitchen for breakfast.

Mama encouraged me to eat a large breakfast, saying, "You'll have a big day. Today, you'll need your strength."

I looked at the two slices of buttered toast and soft boiled egg and quickly lost my appetite. "My stomach is queasy," I said.

"It's nerves," Mama softly replied as she gently placed her arms around me. "You'll do just fine, eat a little, it's OK if you can't finish it all." Mama and Papa took turns and placed their hands on my head to bless me. They both kissed me and wished me good luck. I left the house extra early, and entered the crowded Wilson Avenue Trolley which would bring me to within a few blocks of the school.

I walked briskly to the large building on Irving Avenue. A few students, engaged in lively conversation, stood on the steps to the entrance of the school. I wanted to avoid them; they would ask me too many questions. I tried to appear self-confident; took a deep breath and went inside. I followed other students to the auditorium and sat next to a girl who introduced herself and told me that we would soon be assigned to home rooms. Lucy became my first friend at Bushwick. We promised to go to the movies together the following Sunday.

Late in the afternoon, Mama was full of questions about my first day at school. She noticed that my new white blouse was stained red under the arms. I had been so excited and anxious and perspired so heavily that the red vest leached its color into my blouse. The blouse was a total loss.

Soon I was used to the school routine and welcomed each new challenge. But, I no longer had the luxury of completing my homework assignments when I pleased. Classmates often looked puzzled when I raised my hand to volunteer for extra assignments. I was determined to receive excellent grades, and did not mind doing any additional work to promote my standing in class. I wanted the teachers to notice me. School was a privilege. I had such a fierce battle to reach this point…I was not going to give it up.

I wanted to be known as "the brain" in class, and hoped that my classmates liked me as a person. Therefore, I often volunteered to help them with their homework, and I kept my hand down sometimes, even though I knew the answer to the teacher's question. Still, I heard the whispers. "Here she goes again. She knows it all. She's weird." Those were the last phrases I wanted to hear. I had to be accepted by my peers, not to be isolated again. Therefore, I strove to do well on tests. Here I could outperform my classmates in a not so noticeable fashion. [I recently spoke with a former Bushwick High School classmate who is now a medical doctor. He confessed that he had feared to be in a class with me because of the intense competition I would have created.]

Science became my best subject. To my surprise, I received a hundred percent on my first General Science test, even though my only training in this field was the plant experiment in Miss Kohn's class at Sunshine Cottage. Mr. Ruchlis, the Science Chairman, noticed me, and asked me to help him in his office during my free hour. He trusted me to mark multiple choice tests from his other classes.

Mr. Ruchlis was short and heavy-set. He always had a broad smile. I marvelled at his knowledge and his way of making difficult concepts of science look easy. His enthusiasm was infectious. I looked forward to all of his classes and made sure that I had a front seat. I did not want to miss any part of his demonstrations. Mr. Ruchlis became my hero.

We were encouraged to try out some experiments at home. I recall testing for protein with iodine and accidentally spilling a small drop of iodine on our plastic table cloth, before it hit its designated bean target. I looked with horror at the black spot on the tablecloth. *Papa will surely give me a beating.* Mama came to my rescue. "We'll place a plate over it. See, it's hidden." I was surprised that Mama took it so well. She promised to find a way to get the spot out on another day. Papa never found out about my mishap. From then on, I performed experiments at home very carefully.

The "spot" accident prompted my researching the mechanics of spot removal. Mr. Ruchlis permitted me to use his laboratory at Bushwick. I planned the experiment with proper controls, every day looking for any changes in test tubes containing small pieces of stained and unstained fabric floating in different solvents. Mr. Ruchlis encouraged me to take as many different science courses as possible. I scored high marks in chemistry, biology and physics, and vowed to become a scientist.

I still had to be examined by a doctor every three months and rest a lot. I did all of my reading assignments lying down. Gym classes were off limits for me; too strenuous. I had always liked to participate in gym classes in Germany. Now, in order not to miss sports, I decided to hate them.

When the school issued me an elevator pass, I joined the handicapped students for whom it was too much of a strain to walk up and down the stairs between classrooms. I left class quickly and sneaked to the elevator, hoping not to be seen. I felt ashamed, and I did not want to be known as a sickly person.

I sometimes joined my classmates between classes running up and down the stairs to get to the next class. Many times, the elevator was slow, and I arrived in class late. All eyes were on me during those times, and I felt embarrassed. I pretended nothing was out of the ordinary. Sometimes I ran with the others to get to class. But, I soon realized that walking the stairs tired me out. There was no choice, I had to continue to take the elevator. I made up my mind to be strong and deal with my classmates' stares. Under no circumstance was I going to become sick again.

Even though Mrs. Smith had spent much time with me to correct my pronunciation, I still spoke English with a German accent. There are certain letters like 'v', 'w' and the 'th' sound that are pronounced differently in German. "You have to speak English like a native born American. Watch where I place my tongue. Now, take a mirror and look at yourself when you practice these sounds," said Mrs. Smith. Then, I did not take these exercises too seriously and rarely followed her orders. I was sorry now. Every night I practiced reading aloud. We continued to speak German at home, and our conversations produced a mixture of German and English which would have sounded strange to anyone else. I thought my English sounded more American with each passing day. Two students from Lithuania worked very hard at losing their foreign accents, too. We all wanted to be known as "real Americans," not as "immigrants."

One of my proudest moments was becoming an American citizen. In the spring of 1953, in a Brooklyn Courthouse, I was sworn in with a few other people. The judge told us to raise our right hands, then mumbled a few inaudible words. By the time my hand went down, I was a

Naturalized American citizen. I was surprised how simple the process was. My parents had gone through the process the previous year and they were subjected to an examination consisting of questions about the United States government. I was still a minor and was not tested.

One day, Mr. Ruchlis requested me to stay after class. With much enthusiasm, he said that he wanted to discuss something very important. I became very excited and could hardly wait for the bell to ring to end the period. Then I quickly approached his desk. Mr. Ruchlis said, "There is going to be a City-wide Science Competition. Would you like to be in it? You'll have to do some original research." I answered him immediately, "Of course I do, how can I get started?" Mr. Ruchlis, smiling with approval, said, "Good, I'll give you some ideas. Come to my office tomorrow." I was thrilled to be chosen. I went to his office the following day, and found two other students present. Mr. Ruchlis determined that Andy and Bob would share a project with me. I was a little annoyed that two other students were chosen. I wanted this honor for myself. Mr. Ruchlis recognized my surprise. "Don't worry, all three of you will have enough work to do."

Our project dealt with taking readings of radioactive phosphorus and iodine in different combinations using a Geiger Counter. The clear radioactive substances were poured into long tubes. They looked as if they were filled with water. But, when the Geiger Counter probe touched them, loud clicking was heard. This was an indication of their radioactive state. I spent almost every lunch hour taking readings. We compiled enough data after a few months. We made charts to represent our findings. Andy and Bob gave the presentation at the City-wide Competition held at another high school in Brooklyn. We were thrilled to be awarded a Second Prize in physics! Our award was twenty-five dollars and a certificate. The boys decided to be generous and give me the extra penny; my share was eight dollars and thirty-four cents. I promptly deposited the money in my account at the Roosevelt Savings Bank in Brooklyn.

Extra curricular activities fascinated me. I joined many clubs, and was soon the treasurer of the photography club; associate editor of our newspaper called: "The Bushwick Bulletin;" treasurer of Arista, our honor society; judge on our student court; and member of our chorus. The whole school knew me. I was very happy and had many friends.

I also took part in a City-wide Essay Contest, sponsored by the Chamber of Commerce. One morning, our principal, Dr. Molendyke sent a note to me during a chorus rehearsal. I was to come immediately to her office. I feared the worst. *Would I be expelled from school?* My heart pounded wildly as I entered her office. She spoke with much excitement in her voice. "I am so proud of you. You have won a First Prize in the Chamber of Commerce Essay Contest." I was dumbfounded. Although I tried to speak, no sounds came out of my mouth. After a few seconds I thanked her over and over again. My legs still felt numb and I was afraid of falling. I could hardly wait to tell my parents.

Mama had bought me a new dress on the Lower East Side for the occasion. The award ceremony was held in a large hall of the Chamber of Commerce on Liberty Street in Manhattan. Both of my parents came along. The large room was filled with students, their families, and dignitaries who gave speeches. Each prize winner was introduced and called to the podium. When my turn came, my parents were obviously proud.

As I walked slowly to the podium, I was thinking, *I wonder what the judges would say, if they knew a refugee girl with very little education won this prize.* I'd kept my immigrant story a secret because if they had known my background, they surely would have singled me out for special attention. All essays were judged without the student's identity. *Now, I am just like the others. I did not receive this award out of pity.* After the awards, my parents took me to our favorite Lower East Side restaurant where I ordered a huge plate of french fries and ketchup. The fifteen dollar prize money was deposited into my bank account.

The oldest in my class, and behind in years in schooling, I was embarrassed. Yet, I often thought the reason I did so well in school was because I was older than my classmates and more serious about studies. I was able to complete high school in three instead of four years by going three summers to Washington Irving High School in Manhattan.

Most of Bushwick's students were of Italian descent. Frank, a good looking, heavy-set boy was in most of my classes. He looked older than the other boys, and acted much more mature. Our eyes met often. A few of the girls from my class started to date. Some carried their boyfriend's pictures in their wallets and proudly showed them at every opportunity. Feeling left out and a little jealous of these lucky girls, I decided to encourage Frank. He took the hint and asked me for a date to see "The Great Caruso" at Radio City Music Hall. He was very enthusiastic and proud of the money he had saved from his after school job to take me to a Sunday matinee.

When my father crushed our plans, I was very disappointed. "First of all, you are only fifteen years old," he said. "You can't go out alone with a boy until you are twenty-one. Secondly, he is not Jewish. This could get serious; you are not to marry out of our religion. Don't you remember what those other people did to us? Didn't we suffer enough at their hands?" Papa made me feel terribly guilty, as if the success of the future of the Jewish people was in my hands. Reluctantly I cancelled my date with Frank. I turned on the radio after I came home from school. Elvis Presley, my favorite singer, sang "Heartbreak Hotel." *He must be singing it especially for me.* The words of the song were so appropriate. I cried myself to sleep.

I did have another crush on a boy. Dave was Jewish and one of the smartest students at Bushwick. He had his own column in our school newspaper. I clipped out his picture from the newspaper and placed it in the heart-shaped locket on my bracelet. I never had the courage to flirt with him, I always blushed in his presence, and never dated him.

Soon I felt strong enough to accept a Sunday job as a sales clerk in Mama's Cousin Isi's candy store in Harlem, a part of Manhattan inhabited mainly by Black people. Handing me a broom on my first day, he said, "Sweep up the floor, then you can clean out the display window." I was nervous and I desperately wanted to prove myself a good worker. In my haste to get the display window cleaned, both of my stockings got torn, and one of my legs got a mean scratch. Isi and his wife Anne gradually taught me how to

144

serve ice cream, and sell the other items of the store. But, because I never could do mathematics, I always had trouble giving back the right change to the customers. Even though I made many mistakes, the customers liked me. They gently corrected my errors without complaining to my boss. My salary was seventy-five cents an hour, the minimum wage designated by the government. I tried to be extra polite to the customers. I had heard so many stories of the bad treatment Black people were receiving in the South. I felt sorry for them. I had suffered much in my life because of prejudice. I found it difficult to accept that this was happening in "my America." *It's just not fair. I'll try to do my part and make my customers think of me as a friend, and not just another white-faced girl, who hates them.*

After a few weeks, my parents decided that this job tired me out too much. They advised me to stop working, or risk getting sick again. I had saved at least twenty-five dollars, which, once again, were deposited in my bank account. I was very proud of my earnings and that growing bank account.

My classmates always talked about baseball and because I was a Brooklynite, I thought I should be a Brooklyn Dodgers fan and root for the team at Ebbets Field. I had no idea how the game was played, except that three strikes put a player out of the game. I watched the players run around, catch a ball, throw a ball, and bat at a ball, but I could not get enthusiastic. When the crowd cheered for the Dodgers, also affectionately called the "Bums," I screamed, too. They were our home team. They lost the game on the day of my initiation to baseball. I found the whole experience boring.

Bushwick High School.

Mr. Ruchlis

Science Club, Inge is third from left.

Math Class, Inge (middle) at blackboard.

Photography Club, Inge is third from left.

Senior "Bulletin" Staff hard at work.

Inge, second from right.

Three Bushwick High Students Will Enter 16th Science Fair

To Show Various Radioactivity Experiments In Biology, Chemistry And Physics Fields

Three of Bushwick's atomic energy scientists — Robert Cangemi, Andrew Kovacs and Inge Auerbacher — are planning to show the detection of radioactivity of fissionable metals by the Geiger Counter at the 16th Annual Science Fair. The experimentation project is under the supervision of the science chairman, Mr. Ruchlis.

Geiger Counter In Action

Radioactive lead 210, silver, and sources of gamma rays are being tested for their radioactivity content. The metals are below the danger point of radioactivity and can be safely handled without any harmful effect.

The Science Fair of the American Institute of the City of New York is being sponsored by the Federation of Science Teachers Association of New York with the cooperation of the New York City Public Schools.

Give Cash Prizes

Awards up to $5,000 will be presented to groups, classes and clubs interested in science on the basis of pupil presentations before an audience, science projects, exhibits, experiments or research.

This contest is open to all schools in New York City, from grade 1 through 12. The Presentations will be made on Saturday, December 6, at the Brooklyn Technical High School.

It was disclosed that the three students will present three projects in different fields of science. Experiments dealing with radioactivity in chemistry, biology and physics will be shown.

Article from the Bushwick Bulletin, Novemeber 25, 1952.

Inge and Bob shown.

149

At Summer School

Inge at Washington Irving High School.

CHAPTER SEVENTEEN

Finally Our Own House

Papa and Mama bought a house on 146th Street and 88th Avenue in Jamaica, not far from where cousin Susie lived. My father's cousin Max and his wife Emilie lived on the same block. This was during my last year in high school.

We had searched for a suitable house for a while, but location or price stopped us each time from buying one. Then Cousin Max showed us a house which we knew instantly would become "our house." It was on a block of attached one-family houses and had been owned by a retired high school teacher who had been in poor health for a long time, then suddenly died. Her son, heir to the estate, was anxious to sell the house quickly. We were fortunate to strike a good deal for this little treasure with a pink mimosa tree in front and a small garden in back.

I'd planned to complete my studies at Bushwick, and not transfer to Jamaica High School. I would take the train, or ride with Papa by car to Brooklyn. But, Mama suddenly required costly surgery. This posed a great problem for us. Our finances were very tight since every penny of our savings was needed for the downpayment on the house, and we had no medical insurance. Papa never believed in insurance, except for our car, where it was a legal requirement. "The insurance companies take your money, and when you need them, they don't know you!" he'd said. We came through the crisis with a larger mortgage than originally planned.

While Mama recuperated at Aunt Trudl's and Uncle Karl's new house in Oceanside, Papa and I had the task of moving our belongings from Brooklyn to Jamaica. The biggest problem was my piano. It had to be hoisted out of the living room window. Mrs. Auer watched like a hawk; her only concern was that her house would not be damaged. Papa believed in saving everything. He did not want to discard even useless items. Everything was a "treasure" because it had been such a struggle to acquire each item. Papa was never again going to be told to give up anything as he was in Nazi Germany where everything was taken from us.

I felt very important to suddenly be responsible for so many things. Papa was very nervous, and his temper often flared up. I tried to stay out of his way. I missed Mama. She always knew how to calm both of us. Anger welled up inside of me. *Why did she have to get sick at this time, just when we needed her so much?* Then I immediately felt guilty for having such emotions. Mama would have never deliberately done such a thing. *Mama please forgive me!*

On moving day, Uncle Karl's job was to be the "look-out" so that nothing would be stolen.

We filled the movers' large barrels with dishes, even cracked ones; unnecessary clothes hangers; old clothing, and pots with holes that Mama had saved to possibly be "used for something." I could not imagine these worthless items as other than clutter in our new home. I was relieved when our move went smoothly and was completed.

The inside of the house was neglected and needed a thorough cleaning. I worked very hard at scrubbing the old black kitchen stove and made it shine. The kitchen floor with its accumulated grime was my next target. I became very busy.

Mama recuperated quickly and came home to interior decorate. Our furniture from the Brooklyn apartment was not sufficient to furnish ten empty rooms of our three floor house. Buying furniture would add a new burden to our small bank account.

The house had a large kitchen, dining and living room on the first floor. We moved to the third floor, where the attic had been converted into two bedrooms and a bathroom. The second floor contained two medium sized rooms and a master bedroom, which we later made into two rooms. My parents planned to rent the single rooms of the second floor to individual boarders. This would bring in some money,

Our new home in Jamaica.

and help us pay our mortgage. Each room looked cheerful after Mama furnished it with a vanity, night table, lamp, a bed covered with a colorful chenille bedspread, and a small rug. Yes, Mama was ready for the boarders, too. She had gotten advice from our neighbors who rented rooms to boarders and from Max and Emilie, who warned her against women who caused too much trouble; wanted to cook in your kitchen and messed up so much; let their wet laundry drip all over the floor; and got cold cream on everything! She anxiously taped a sign on the front door which read, "Room for rent, inquire within."

CHAPTER EIGHTEEN

The Boarders

Next morning, the doorbell rang and Mama opened the door to a man and a woman. The woman asked, "Do you have a room for rent?" Mama countered, "Is it for a couple?" "No, but we are looking for a room for someone very special to us. You see, we are planning to adopt a baby, and we heard of a young lady from the Mid-West who is pregnant and wants to give up her baby for adoption. I am sure my husband, who is a dentist, and I can give the baby a good home. This young lady will live here until the baby is born. You don't have to worry, we'll pay for everything," the woman replied. Mama hesitated; Emilie did tell her not to accept women. But, suppose no one else would come for a room and we'd missed this opportunity. We needed the money. So, Mama took a deep breath and agreed to accept her. Mama was going to take care of the rooms and household and help Papa build his business. Both would come home late every night. I was to help with housework on weekends.

Marlene came the following day. She carried a suitcase in one hand and in the other an overnight bag. Mama liked her instantly. I was very excited to meet Marlene, and went upstairs to introduce myself after coming home from school. I had expected a much older woman. She did not look pregnant, her tall figure was still slim. She had long straight blond hair, which surrounded a face of Nordic features. Her eyes were pale blue, and she had a warm smile. She even had my favorite doll's name. We were close in age and soon became good friends. It was wonderful having someone my own age in the house. We had many long talks together, and although I was curious, I never had the courage to question her about her past. *Did her husband leave her, was she unmarried? How did she meet the couple from New York City?* I concluded that she must have had terrible problems to make the drastic decision to give up her baby.

As time went on, Marlene's stomach began to bulge. We never spoke about the baby, only about her "condition." "When my 'condition' is over, I'll go home again," she'd say. She surprised me with a gift one evening, a pair of sunglasses with dark green frames. Marlene said, smiling, "They'll look good on you, and will compliment your dark brown hair and olive complexion."

The couple kept their promise paying Marlene's rent and calling up a few times to inquire about her health. They never came to see her. The few months passed quickly and then Marlene went to the hospital to have her baby. Mama and I visited her in the hospital and brought her a gift. We inquired about her baby girl. Marlene was not allowed to see her. *How awful to carry a baby for nine months and feel its presence inside your body, go through the pains of childbirth, and never be able to touch and see it.* Yet, she did not look sad. After we said good-bye to Marlene, we never heard from her or the couple again. I often wondered if years later she had any regrets about her final decision and longed for her daughter.

There were many more boarders during the next twenty years. Some had unique stories, and we became close friends with a few. Countess von der Recke was one of these special people who touched our hearts. Her son saw our advertisement for a furnished room in the newspaper and came to inquire. He looked very distinguished and spoke with a German accent. He was thrilled that he stumbled upon such good luck to find the perfect home for his elderly, divorced mother. She was living with him, his wife and two young sons for a short time in a very crowded apartment within walking distance from our house.

Countess von der Recke looked older than her sixty years. Her hair was snow-white. She was of medium height and appeared rather frail. Although her clothing looked almost shabby, her regal manner gave away that she had seen better days. We were requested not to call her "Countess," but address her as simply "Mrs." "There is no royalty in America, everyone is the same here," she said. She became part of the family and took part in our celebrations and company dinners. She never flaunted her former riches or family background, and remained almost too humble in our presence. Her son continued to pay her rent, since she was penniless. She worked some hours doing housework in nearby houses to earn a few dollars before Christmas, and be able to buy gifts for her grandchildren.

I spent many hours sitting on her bed listening to her many stories. There was an extra bonus, too. She could read cards and I often pursuaded her to tell my fortune.

Mrs. von der Recke came from a small town in Eastern Germany where her family owned a huge castle and much land. She could trace her royal family tree back many hundreds of years. Her father was often a guest at the court of the King and Queen of England. She knew many intimate details of numerous members of Europe's royalty. It was fascinating to have history come alive, and to hear about things that were never publicized or written about in books. One day she showed me a set of silverware engraved with the family's coat of arms. This was her only keepsake of her entire fortune and she guarded it with her life. She also had a personal letter sent to her from Queen Mary of Great Britain. Her hometown was occupied by the Russian Army during World War II, and her castle was confiscated. It was later used as a school. Mrs. von der Recke had one son, and was divorced from her husband, who also belonged to the German nobility. She and her son made their way to the American occupied zone after World War II. Then Germany was sliced up into four occupied zones: the American,

Countess von der Recke.

British, French, and Russian areas. Mrs. von der Recke's son met and later married a coal miner's daughter, who was a member of the American Armed Forces. Mrs. von der Recke was not pleased with this strange match for her handsome young son. The couple was soon permitted to come to America. Mrs. von der Recke was able to join them here later.

Mrs. von der Recke lived with us for a few years, until her son's separation from his wife. Then she moved back to her son's apartment to live with him. Her stay was short, she died soon afterwards from a heart attack. We never forgot her and sometimes visit her grave which is in a nearby cemetery.

Another boarder made a lasting impression on me. It was not so much the person as his story. Joseph was employed as an electrical engineer, a "trouble shooter" for a large company. As we got to know him better, he confided in us that he was chosen to inspect the electric chair in the Sing Sing Prison in Ossining, New York, after the Rosenbergs were put to death by electrocution in it. The Rosenberg spy case caused much hysteria and excitement in 1951. Julius, a minor government employee and his wife, Ethel, were charged with treason for giving America's Atomic secrets to Russia. During World War II, the Russians had fought side by side with the Americans. They had had a common goal—to rid the world of Nazism. But the Russians soon began a dangerous campaign to spread the Communist doctrine. Like their German predecessors, they were determined to gain control of large areas of the world. Instead of Nazism, they wanted to force Communism on the people of many lands. After World War II, America and

Russia became bitter enemies over their different political ideologies. The "Cold War" began.

The United States felt safe from a Russian attack, since it claimed a monopoly on the Atomic bomb. Reports came to the White House in the fall of 1949 that Russia had exploded an atomic device. Questions arose. "How did the Russians make the bomb so quickly? Were there spies in America?" The Russians were considered backward in this advanced technology; someone must have leaked important information to them. Americans became fearful of an Atomic attack. Bomb shelters were built. School children and adults were trained in civil defense and survival methods. I remember hearing the shrill sound of the siren blasting its warning signal during my early high school years. We were trained to cower under our desks and cover our eyes. Most of my fellow students did not take these survival drills very seriously. They had never before experienced the ravages of war. Wars were always fought far from home. I knew too well what war was like and became very frightened. When I heard the familiar sound of the wailing warning siren, I broke out in a cold sweat. The terror returned. The Rosenbergs were held responsible for the casualties of the Korean War, too. On June 25, 1950, North Korean Communists, aided and trained by the Russians, crossed the 38th Parallel and invaded South Korea. The "Cold War" between the United States and the Soviet Union became "hot." The judge sentenced the Rosenbergs to death. He concluded, if Russia had not owned the Atomic bomb, she would not have gotten involved in the Korean conflict and given support to the Korean Communists. The Rosenbergs were executed in 1953, although they claimed their innocence of treason until their last breaths. Ethel and Julius Rosenberg had two young sons. I felt great sadness for these two innocent victims who became orphans.

Our boarders came from many countries. One good looking, dark haired young man told us that he was a cousin of Soroya, who was then wife of the Shah of Iran. He was a student in his native country and got involved in activities and demonstrations against the Shah's policies. He was black-listed and left Iran in fear of his life.

We had one light blond-haired student from Iceland. He was studying to become an airport traffic controller. An older man from Puerto Rico was very religious and in secret lit many candles in his room, although he was told not to do so because he could start a fire. Nick, a Greek and former sailor was at one time chief steward on a famous Greek shipping owner's private yacht. He told us of the parties on board and of the famous people who attended them. He even had clues to an unsolved murder that took place aboard the yacht. He said, "I know everything that went on, but if I talk, I am dead."

All potential boarders tried to make a good first impression when they rented the room. Some of the male boarders had serious drinking problems, and came home drunk at night. They stumbled up the stairs and woke us up. Sometimes they soiled the bed, and those who smoked often burned holes into the small rug near their bed and left tell-tale black burn marks on our furniture. Mama talked to them in the morning, "Either you change your ways, or you'll have to leave! This is a nice house, and we don't want drunks here!" Each one promised to change his ways, but when each repeated his actions, he was told to pack his belongings and leave. One of the boarders suddenly left in the middle of the night, and a room became empty. Mike came the same day that we put out our vacancy sign. It was a lucky break for me. He was nineteen years old, single and Jewish. We became friends.

My high school studies were coming to an end. Everyone was talking about the Senior Prom and the Senior Play. I made sure that I had a part in the play; the stage and acting held a special attraction for me. But the prom posed a big problem. No one had asked me to be his date. I was getting desperate. Many of my friends had the same problem. I was determined to find someone. This was one occasion that I was not going to miss.

I told Mike about the prom. He took the hint and offered to take me. I was very proud to be escorted by an "older man." All my friends' eyes were on us as we danced until dawn at the Boulevard Night Club in Forest Hills, Queens.

Then came graduation. I proudly accepted many honors, among them the coveted Excellence in Biology Certificate. Our graduation song, "You'll Never Walk Alone," became my theme for life. Dressed in black cap and gown, I joined my classmates in singing, "When you walk through a storm, hold your head up high, and don't be afraid of the dark." These words hammered their message inside my brain; always be positive, even when everything goes wrong. There was a golden sky after the storm. For the first time in my life, I completed a school program. I had to pinch myself. It was real!

High School Prom—1953. Inge (seated) second from right.

Inge's High School graduation portrait, 1953.

CHAPTER NINETEEN

They Shoot Horses

The summer of 1953 was wonderful. I was eighteen years old. I joined a Jewish youth group and met many boys. Sometimes, I went on two dates in one day, dancing half the night, and seeing many plays and movies. My weight finally dropped and I was popular with the boys.

I attended many beach parties and thought that I looked sexy in my bathing suit. But, a dark cloud, a constant reminder of my past illness, hung over me. Exposure to the sun was considered dangerous for people in my state of health at that time. The doctors claimed that the sun's ultra violet rays could break down the defense barriers against the tubercle bacillus. My doctor warned me to stay out of the strong rays of the sun, or, if I insisted on sunbathing, to always cover myself. Mama bought me a white, sleeveless terry cloth jacket. I was ashamed to wear it. I was tired of telling my friends that I wore it to avoid getting a sun burn. They never wore anything over their bathing suits, and I was often teased about looking funny with my cover-up. They often said, "What are you hiding underneath?" I felt out of place. But then I swallowed my pride and ignored their silly comments. I was having too good a time, and I would not let them spoil it.

Summer ended too soon and the great new challenge of college began. I entered Queens College of the City University system in Flushing, Queens as a Pre-Medical student with the hope of becoming a medical doctor. I was surrounded most of my life by doctors, and this seemed a logical choice. I wanted to pursue a career that combined science with social service.

Everyone at Queens College entered with a high grade average. The competition was keen. I no longer had the "super star" status that I enjoyed at Bushwick. It was difficult to compete with all the others, who also had been "stars" in their schools before coming to Queens.,

By this time I had made up my mind to marry a doctor. It became an obsession. Because of my medical history, I searched for someone who I believed would have a better understanding of my past. He would know how to properly take care of me. The man in white became a god-like symbol to me.

I had been careful about answering all the questions on the college application. I halted when I saw the questions, "Have you ever had a serious illness? Have you ever been hospitalized? Explain each!" My first reaction was to skip them. If there were any questions later on, I could always say, "I must have over-looked them." But, my conscience bothered me. I answered the questions in an almost illegible scrawl. I was afraid that the college would not accept me, because of my health history. There was an additional burden. All entering students were required to have a chest X-ray.

After a few weeks at Queens, I received a letter from the college requesting me to see my private doctor for more tests. The college doctor had found my X-ray suspicious. I was furious. How dare a machine reveal my deepest secret!

I feared the worst, since there were familiar warning-signs. I was unusually tired most of the day, and had lost too much weight. My doctor's verdict was straight to the point. "You must have exhausted yourself during the summer—you are sick again!" Those words fell on me like a hot branding iron. I was stunned and hurt. I pounded my fists into my pillow at night. Hot tears of anger and frustration flowed down my cheeks. *No, no this can't be happening.* I was glad that my bedroom door was closed because I did not want my parents to hear my sobbing. They must have been devastated by the news, too. I did not want to add to their grief. *Am I to be cursed the rest of my life with this sickness?*

My college career ended after only six weeks at Queens. I was ordered back to bed and placed on three different drugs; a combination of twenty-six pills, and two injections every day. The doctor had decided to use every known drug for TB to finally end my misery.

This chemotherapy made me very sick and I could barely eat anything. I was constantly nauseous and did not want to fight this evil giant anymore. *I wanted to die!* Life seemed over for me. What was the use to go to war and lose the battle every time?

One day, a young male boarder from the next house came looking for a room for a friend. He noticed me and began a conversation. Murray was twenty-six years old and Jewish. He had dark-brown hair and was very handsome. We became close friends. He visited me every weekend and surprised me each time with something special, like a new book or record. Our relationship was soon more than just friendship. We fell in love. He noticed the large jar filled with pills next to my bed. I told him they were vitamins, because I was afraid to tell him the truth and lose him. No one wants a sick girlfriend. I covered my mouth when he wanted to kiss me to protect him from catching my disease. "One day soon we'll do it," I told him.

I found joy in life again. I wanted to live and fight the sickness. The wonder medicine was working and I was not feeling constantly nauseous anymore.

These are two poems I wrote reflecting the forces of death, life and love that I was facing all at once at that time:

Death

When will God's finger point at me,
to climb the golden ladder,
And enter the gate of eternity.
Time has wings and time can fly.
Till the last minute has ticked away,
I shall lie down to rest and die.

Not before, shall I think of such things,
Of human sorrow and heartaches,
Which to you death brings.
My life must be happy and gay,
For life is short and sweet,
And light as a day in May.

I must love you with all my heart,
We shall always stay together,
'Till death do us part.
But, I will await you in some foreign land,

Hoping, praying to see you again,
I will greet you there with an outstretched hand.

Sail to me to some faraway shore.
As soon as Death grants it,
That we may join our love forevermore.

The Pill of Life

I hold within my hands a life,
A life with all its worth.
I hold within this pill,
The greatest treasure on earth.

There lies a shell in my hand,
Hiding magic power from view,
A miniature bomb in all its glory,
Disguised by capsule and hue.

This great weapon fights a war each day,
Emitting strange power from within.
And turning death's march another way,
That another life be spared again.

One of my pills was a giant, red capsule and inspiration for
the foregoing poem.

♦   ♦   ♦

My relationship with Murray ended after a few months.
He simply told me one day that he had kept a secret from me.

He was married and had rented the room next door when he separated from his wife. Now, they had come to an understanding and reconciled their differences. He was returning to his wife. I was angry and heart-broken and kept my own secret locked away. *I should not be so hard on him. We both were not honest with each other.*

A year passed before I could resume studies at Queens. My friends kept me posted of their activities at college. They had joined many clubs and were having a good time. I envied them!

For so long I had tried so hard to catch up with my studies. Now I was behind again. I now knew that the physical strain would not allow me to become a doctor, but I continued my studies in science with my new goal of a Bachelor of Science degree in chemistry and work one day in medical research.

Louise was also attending Queens, majoring in English. It was early December, and neither of us had a New Year's Eve date yet and we were getting desperate. I wanted to go to a dance sponsored by a Jewish Singles Club in Manhattan and begged Louise to go, too. "I have a Latin exam coming up, I have to study," she said. Disappointed but determined, I decided to go alone. I bought a pair of dangling silver-like earrings at Woolworth as a declaration of purpose. *Louise will be so jealous, if I meet someone.*

There was a five dollar cover charge to enter the crowded dance hall. I was ready with freshly polished finger nails, new "silver" earrings, and my glasses off. "Boys don't make passes at girls who wear glasses," were serious words. Whenever I attended an important function, I would automatically remove my glasses, and make sure to do so in time so no one present would know that I wore them. If I was on a movie date I would feel my way in the darkness to my seat, and only then put on my glasses. As soon as the film was over, I removed them. In the dance hall, I had to strain my eyes to see better, and hoped that they would not cross without the glasses. Couples dancing the jitterbug were a stream of color, and the band was loud. I moved in place to the pulsating rhythm. *I hope someone will ask me to dance.* Then to make myself visible to a potential partner, I walked from one end of the hall to the other. I was approached before too long.

Henry introduced himself in a heavy, accented English. He was not much taller than I, but tall enough to offset my self-consciousness about my height. He had dark blond hair, a warm-broad smile and generally looked rather handsome. We danced all night and he took me home. We planned a date for the following Saturday night, and spoke on the telephone almost every day. We liked each other and began dating. I knew Henry had serious intentions when he took me home to meet his parents and married sister. They lived in the lower middle-class section of Brownsville in Brooklyn. They seemed to like me. Henry and his family were Polish. They had escaped the Nazi terror in Poland and spent the war years in Siberia, a desolate area in what was then the Soviet Union.

To celebrate my twenty-first birthday, Henry invited me to a New Year's Eve party at a Russian night club. The night before the big event, I decided to have a serious talk with Mama. Henry had been speaking more and more about marriage, and I had so many questions. I was afraid of the responsibility marriage would bring. I would have to share my bed with him. What would this be like? Mama had always warned me never to let a man take advantage of me. She always reminded me of purity. "Don't ever permit a man to touch your private parts. Remember, you have to be a virgin when you marry," she would say. And what would childbirth be like? Everyone spoke of the awful pain that had to be endured. Pain was the last thing I wanted. I had enough of it in the past. There was also my sickness. I asked Mama whether I should speak to Henry about it. I thought that when people marry they must share everything, know all about each other's lives. Surely, Henry must have great understanding for human beings, since as a veterinarian he shows such compassion for animals.

Mama's answer was quick and to the point. "Sweetheart, no one is perfect in this world. Remember one fact. When two people really love each other, they accept each other's frailties and tolerate each other's faults. That is the real test for real love beyond sexual attraction."

Mama's words sounded like a sermon a rabbi might give in the synagogue. When she completed her short speech, I had the answer to my question. I would be honest and test Henry's love for me.

I knew it was going to be a special night and I was not surprised when Henry proposed. I told him of my health background. He was shocked. The next day he acted very cold and cancelled an ice-skating date with me. I called him up and pleaded with him to speak to my physician. He was reluctant, but finally agreed to a private meeting with the doctor. I remained alone in the waiting room, nervously biting my nails and walking around the room. I strained against the silence to hear what they were saying, but the office door was shut tight. I could feel my heart beating very fast. Waiting was agony. *What are they discussing? It's taking so long. I can't breathe!*

I was startled when the door opened. Henry looked grim. My heart knew that Henry had made up his mind. He spoke very little when he took me home. "Good-bye Inge, I wish you good luck," he said, and left me standing in front of my house. He walked briskly towards the subway station. Our relationship was over.

Devastated, I cried for weeks.... My parents and friends offered support.... My grades suffered.... *He is treating me like an animal that has tuberculosis. Horses may get shot when they become ill, but I am a human being! I am cured! I am a normal person again!* I had certainly tested Henry's love for me...!

Soon afterwards, I consulted my doctor who talked with me in a fatherly way. "He didn't deserve you. Don't worry, you will find someone who will appreciate and love you for who you are," he reassured me. He was convincing, and I wanted to believe his words.

Time heals. I dated other people. Then I changed colleges and spent one semester at New York University where I met, in a Qualitative Chemistry class, an Arab from Jordan. Both of our last names started with A. Said was very handsome, and I was very attracted to his dark features, his tall build, and exotic-smelling shave lotion. Everything he touched smelled of this exotic scent.

Over apple pie and coffee after school I asked Said if he hated me. "We are supposed to be enemies," I proclaimed. He answered instantly, "Our historical background is very similar. We are Semites. Abraham is our grandfather, so we are cousins." We concluded that we were in fact more alike than different; that political leaders made government policies to divide countries and people.

When I returned to Queens College, I kept as a souvenir a pencil that Said had lent me. It still smelled of his perfume. I would never forget him.

Four years of college were consumed with long hours of study and making new friends. I attended many House Plan parties at Queens. Membership in a House Plan was cheaper than in a Sorority, and it was easier to join. We were all under pressure from our parents to meet someone and get married soon after graduation. I proudly clung to my Bachelor of Science degree in chemistry when I graduated from Queens College in June, 1958.

Years of medical research with prominent doctors at major hospitals followed. During this time I concluded that doctors were only human beings and had no more compassion or understanding than anyone else. I had met a doctor specializing in Physical Medicine, a field dealing with the disabilities which could be helped by physical therapy and rehabilitation. He proposed to me after a few weeks, but rejection followed once I told him of my dark secret. He was a Jew born in Iraq where there was still a stigma against people like myself.

The Youth Group: 1953

Inge, top row, on left.

Inge, on left.

Graduation from Queens College, 1958.

Inge working as a chemist.

175

Inge.

CHAPTER TWENTY

The Return

As the years went by, the past sank into the canyons of memory. I wanted to block out the bad years of my childhood and fully adopt America as my new homeland. America had been good to me; nursing me back to good health, giving me the chance for a new life filled with endless possibilities. I tried to lose my German accent so that I would not be branded as a foreigner and I rarely spoke to anyone about my past. That was something that happened thousands of miles away in another time.

One day while watching a television program about a Czech woman survivor returning to the Terezin concentration camp to show her teenage daughter where she was imprisoned as a child, I, too, suddenly felt the need to return to the places of my childhood. The sleeping volcano erupted.

I went back to Sunshine Cottage in 1966 and found the building empty of patients. It was now used as a hospital teaching facility. The "Boys End" of Ward 200 still had beds and looked the same as when I had left it. But the other areas of the ward were converted into classrooms. Polio and tuberculosis, two dreaded diseases of my time had almost disappeared.

A few months later I returned to Europe to see with adult eyes what I had experienced as a child. Why did I want to remember those miserable days? I believed I was searching for a deeper understanding of my own life.

In Germany I visited my mother's hometown—Jebenhausen, a place associated with the happiest times of my childhood. I went to see some familiar families, but could not recognize anybody. All of us had grown older. My best friend Elisabeth now was married and the mother of two little blond daughters. I visited the farmers who risked their lives giving us food in the darkest days of the Nazi era. Then I went to the Jewish cemetery to see my grandfather's grave and tears rolled down my cheeks as I touched the cold grey tombstone and wondered about Grandma. *Poor Grandma, if only she could have found a peaceful resting place, too. Where is her grave? Where is the unmarked ditch in a dark forest of Latvia.* I felt Grandma's presence and thought I heard her quiet words of comfort, "Don't cry my child; I am at peace, pursue your dreams and be happy!"

At the Christian cemetery in Jebenhausen I placed a flower on Therese's grave. She was my grandmother's maid for twenty-five years and was killed by an American soldier at the war's end. The soldier thought that she was hiding ammunition in her house and shot through the door. She had not heeded his command to surrender both out of fear and lack of understanding English. Therese was loyal to us in the worst days of hatred against the Jewish people. She came in the middle of the night to bring us food, and saved some of our prayer books and family photo albums. If only more Germans were like her, the Holocaust would never have happened.

I also visited my hometown—Kippenheim. I walked in front of our house, but I did not enter. Some of the streets looked familiar. The synagogue, which was partially destroyed on November 9, 1938 during the riot called "Kristallnacht," when most of the synagogues of Germany and Austria were destroyed, now served as a storage house for animal feed. I spoke briefly to some people and then took a taxi to the Jewish cemetery in the nearby village of Schmieheim where Papa's parents rested. I never knew them, for they had died before my parents' marriage. This cemetery looked neglected in contrast to the one in Jebenhausen, where the local government insured proper care. Some gravestones had been overturned and vandalized. The grass appeared to have been uncut for a long time. My grandparents' graves seemed in order. I gently touched the rough stones and followed the Jewish custom of remembrance, placing a small stone on each. Frozen in front of their graves, I spoke to them in a soft voice. "Grandpa and Grandma, I am really sorry that I never knew you. But, in a way, you were lucky not to be alive during those awful years. I hate to think what could have happened to you." Did they hear my words? Chirping birds broke the silence and I welcomed the change in mood. I walked toward the entrance of the cemetery and paused in front of the War Memorial for the fallen Jewish soldiers of World War I. I saw our family name listed among the victims. We had been recognized loyal German citizens. How, then, could such a tragedy have befallen us? I could not understand....

Townspeople greeted me with friendship. They claimed that they personally were always against the Nazi regime and never hated the Jews. I left them with mixed feelings. The policemen wearing peaked hats reminded me of the brutal

Nazi SS officers. Although they were courteous and really did not scream at me, hearing the German language from their mouths evoked fear. When we speak German at home, it sounds differently, and I associate our German with the warm feelings of home and of my grandparents, not war and orders.

I stopped in Prague, Czechoslovakia. It was raining and the dismal weather reflected my mood as I began a journey into the darkest time of my past. The Bohemian countryside flew by during the short bus ride from Prague. Large fields, small towns and direction, markers awakened memories: Bohusovice, Litmerice, and finally Terezin. After a two-hour ride a sign in Terezin directed "To the Memorial and Crematory."

The bus stopped near the old market place and I got off. Suddenly, a noisy group of children passed by and I imagined myself in their midst. Yes, this is what it was like when I was a small child. The only difference was that then they were Jewish children, and most of them would be exterminated. Slowly, more memories awakened by the sight of familiar houses and streets. At one time, Terezin was a military garrison, then it was converted by the Nazis into a concentration camp. Much had changed during the passage of time. The small stores which had served as our living quarters were open for business again. The barracks were occupied by Czech soldiers and off limits to all visitors. Some of the former inhabitants of Terezin had returned to their homes. In 1941 all the people of Terezin were ordered by the Nazis to leave their houses to make room for the Jewish prisoners. Now, there was even a small hotel, where one could eat quite well. I ordered breaded mushrooms.

What would we have given during those awful days for just a piece of bread?

Across from the Dresdner Kaserne, a large Army barrack, were the Q-808 and Q-806 houses in which we once lived. I mustered courage and rang one of the bells. I was curious about who was living there now. An elderly woman opened the door, and when I explained, she understood my need to visit. She and her husband owned this home before their eviction in 1941. They returned in 1947.

As I stood in that tiny room which had housed six persons on double-deck bunk-beds, memories hung on my shoulders. There was no other furniture then; only the ugly beds made of unpolished wood, infested with fleas and bedbugs. We had shared these quarters with Ruth and her parents. Tears flowed as I recalled the talented child whose life was so cruelly terminated in 1944, just before her tenth birthday, in the gas chambers at Auschwitz. Now, the room seemed peaceful. Windows had been added to the previously dark quarters.

I remembered that there had been a bake-oven in a back room. The elderly woman told me that my memory was correct. The bakery was never opened again. Now the space was a bedroom.

I walked to the back alley which had served as our playground. Not much had changed. It was still cluttered with refuse, the outdoor toilet was still in use—and probably rat-infested. The smell of human waste was still in the air. I recalled when birds made a nest high up in a house above this alley. How I envied them. They could fly away from all the misery, while we were "walled" in.

Then I made my way to the City Hall, which had served formerly as the Nazi SS Headquarters. We had been forbidden to walk on the street leading to it. Suddenly, it was 1942 again, and I was seven years old, holding my doll in my arms. Fear gripped my heart as I climbed the stairs to meet the Mayor of Terezin in his office. I introduced myself. He was surprised to see such a young survivor, and asked me many questions. The Mayor treated me with respect and great warmth. He had been appointed some years before, and seemed happy in this position, although he was old enough to have vivid memories of the evil associated with this town. He offered to drive me to the Small Fortress, which is used as a museum now. The Small Fortress had belonged to the Terezin complex, but it was a military prison and had its own SS Commandant. It also served as a place of extra punishment for any misconduct we in the large fortress might have committed. Our accountable crimes were such things as stealing potatoes, or being caught drawing a picture of the "real" conditions of the camp. The Small Fortress had solitary confinement cells and an area for firing squads. It was a brutal place that was feared as much as being sent to "the East." We then drove to the Crematory.

I realized, as I stood in the Crematory near the ovens that had burned thousands of dead bodies, that I carried a tremendous responsibility. My life was not to be lived in vain. It was to be my duty now to speak out against prejudice, and to continue my life with a more challenging and meaningful career in the name of so many innocent victims who I must represent. I continued along the walk to the Memorial and Cemetery. Red flowers bloomed here as a symbol of our martyrs' spilled blood. My next destination was the L-235 house on Bahnhofstrasse (Train Street), which was our last living quarter. We were liberated from here by the Soviet Army on May 8, 1945. But, not before almost being hit with hand grenades thrown into the camp by the fleeing Nazis. I continued on Train Street and found a short section of railroad tracks overgrown with grass. It had started to rain. I pushed the grass aside to touch the cold, wet railroad ties. From this spot there had been no hope; the next stop was Auschwitz. I felt that the cold steel I was touching was a line to eternity and I imagined I heard the heartbeats and screams of innocent men, women and children whose lives would be snuffed out as the doors of the cattle cars closed.

Since I felt physically strong again, I decided, after my return to America, to follow my dream and apply to Medical School. There was one problem. I was thirty-one years old, too old for admission to an American school at that time. But schools in Europe accepted older students and I decided on a German-speaking country. (Switzerland had closed its doors to most foreign students.) I chose Heidelberg University in Germany even though my friends and my parents discouraged me from going there, because of my traumatic history. I went ahead and applied for admission to their Medical School, and to my great surprise was accepted.

In the spring of 1968 I left my job as a chemist in a hospital laboratory. I flew to Germany and rented a room in Wieblingen, a village near Heidelberg. Next I travelled to Stuttgart to have my college credits evaluated. The German medical school program was six years long and I wanted to save myself two years of schooling, since I already had completed all of my Pre-Medical training in America. When a secretary in the Stuttgart Admission's Office asked me why I returned to Germany and did not continue my studies in the United States, I caught her tone of voice and read between the lines. What she meant was that I was taking a German student's place for the study of medicine. She had my application in front of her, and obviously knew that I was Jewish. I was stunned by her attitude and returned to Wieblingen. The next day was May 1st, a holiday celebrated in Germany. Loud singing was coming from a short distance away from where I lived. Night had fallen on a festive day, and the villagers wanted to continue the merriment. I opened the shutters of my window to better hear and see what was going on. The villagers were not singing old German folk songs, they were singing brutal Nazi songs! I could not believe my ears! I handed in my resignation to study medicine the following day, just before the spring semester was to begin.

I heard-church bells chiming They were tolling for me. My dream of becoming a doctor had ended. Later, I spoke to Jewish students at Heidelberg who were happy and comfortable studying there. Even if my incidents were unfortunate or atypical, they changed the direction of my career forever.

Inge and the Mayor of Terezin in front of Crematorium, 1966.

CHAPTER TWENTY-ONE

Beyond the Yellow Star

With great satisfaction I continue to work as a chemist in a hospital laboratory. I have my own special obligation to help preserve life, not work in ways to destroy it.

During the Holocaust, one and a half million Jewish children were slaughtered. I feel those three million eyes haunting and pleading with me not to forget them. I am dedicating most of my free time to lecturing at schools, universities, churches, synagogues, libraries and other community service organizations. I have made it my mission to use my life spreading the message that only brotherhood and education can prevent events such as The Holocaust from happening again.

My greatest joy is to enter a classroom or an auditorium filled with young people and teachers. Many times it is a special assembly. The children are noisy, and are fidgeting in their seats. They seem anxious and a little bewildered about what they will hear. I look into a field of humanity made up of individuals from many ethnic backgrounds. It is like a large bouquet of an assortment of wild flowers, each with its distinct color and design. I see the Indian Sikh boy with his long hair tucked under the small white piece of cloth on top of his head, the Black girl with her corn-row hairdo, the Jewish boy wearing his skull cap, the Oriental girl playing with her straight black hair, and the Irish freckle-faced boy with flaming red hair. They all blend into each other and are only separated by the boundaries of their

186

seats. I gaze at this human rainbow and wonder what brought these children's families or ancestors to America? From what oppression, poor living conditions or danger did they flee? America is so different from many other countries; She is our mother whose open arms offer a safe haven from the many hells of the world.

The principal is at the microphone introducing me. There is total silence. All eyes are on me. Some of the lights are turned off as I begin my slide presentation. The children's eyes are fixed on the projected pictures. I watch their facial expressions as my story unfolds. Many wipe a tear away, embarrassed to be caught. The little red-haired boy blows his nose trying to appear grown up by hiding behind his tissue. I feel sad and a little guilty for moving impressionable youngsters to tears, but, if I do not evoke any emotion, my presentation would have no meaning. I show the last slide. The lights go on. I reassure the children that it is OK to be touched by my story; even to cry a little. I tell them, "We have to feel what can happen to humanity when evil people come to power; when innocent people are blamed for anything that goes wrong in a country." There is still a hush in the room. The children remain frozen in their seats. I sense an uneasiness in the crowd, and I must break the silence. I continue, "I am sure many of you have questions to ask. Please, don't be afraid to speak up."

The children begin to move around in their seats. A blond boy raises his hand and asks in an almost inaudible voice, "Why didn't you fight back?" I answer him without hesitation, "That is a question people of all age groups ask me. At first it bothered me. I used to think, how dare anyone ask such a question. It was as if to say that we were cowards and went like sheep to the slaughter. Yes, we outnumbered our enemy by many thousands of people, but most of us did not have any weapons. Our bodies were weak from lack of food. Our spirits were broken from the humiliation, torture, and isolation we had to endure. Just to live one more day was our weapon to fight back. The Nazis wanted all Jews to die, but we resisted them with all the strength we had left to stay alive. For me, the fact that I saved my doll was like fighting with a gun."

The children are inspired by the courage of the little boy. Suddenly the auditorium is alive with raised hands. Almost everyone is anxious to ask a question. "Have you ever seen Hitler?"

"Did you ever try to run away?"

"Were you scared?"

"What happened to your doll?"

I answer each question. "No, I never saw Hitler. Yes, I was often scared. I kept my doll Marlene 'till some time ago, when I donated her to the United States Holocaust Memorial Museum in Washington, D.C. to be shared with all people. To me she will always be a symbol of humanity, of the warm memories of home and my beloved Grandmother, who gave her to me. It was hard for me to make the decision to give her up. Marlene was the only object I saved from my childhood. She must serve as a warning against bigotry. You can visit her in Washington."

A tall Black boy stands up and speaks in a strong, steady voice. "I'm an African American, why should all this concern me? My people came here as slaves, and we suffered much since then. This is supposed to be America, and not Nazi Germany."

I took a deep breath before answering. I had expected such a question. So, I began, "All hatred based on racism and ethnic background is wrong, and must not be tolerated. No child is born with hate. Hate is an acquired behavior. The reason I am here today, is to show you to what extent people will go to make evil a religion. It is wrong for people to mistreat each other because they are different in color or ethnic background. Hitler believed that all Jews had to be eliminated because their blood was inferior to that of the German people. He said: 'Jewish blood would pollute the German Master Race.' The truth is that all blood types occur in all races and all nations. When we need a blood transfusion we need only to be sure that we are receiving the blood type compatible with ours. The origin of the blood is never identified. It does not matter whether it came from a Black, White, Hispanic or Oriental donor. Never in modern history has there been outright murder on such a scale as Hitler's war against the Jews in Europe. I am here today to help you fight bigotry, and to make you more sensitive towards other human beings, who may look different from you. Remember, we all belong to the same family of Man. We must never have another Holocaust!"

The Black boy is not completely satisfied with my answer and continues, "That's all very nice for a White person to say. You can always hide behind your skin."

I answer him: "You are right about my color, but during the war I had to wear a yellow star that branded me as a Jew. I wore that badge of shame with honor. One should be proud of his or her heritage, no matter what people say."

The last questions came from a male teacher standing in the back of the auditorium. "Do you hate the Germans, today? What gave you the strength to survive, and be the positive person you appear to be today?"

"My answer to your first question is yes, I certainly hate the people who were involved in these horrible crimes. But, I will not blame Germans growing up today for the heinous deeds of their grandparents. Hate is negative energy and does no one any good.

"In answer to your second question: My survival from the concentration camp depended on chance and luck. When the last selection to Auschwitz was made in 1944, a red circle had been drawn around our names. We had been spared from certain death in the gas chamber. I also attribute my survival to the good fortune of being permitted to remain with my parents most of the time. They did their best to shelter me from the blows, ease my pain, and still my hunger and fears in the presence of great odds. They gave me much support and help to become a productive person."

I am often asked if the concentration camp experience has changed me emotionally? "No survivor can say that his psyche is completely in tact after experiencing such devastation and humiliation. My parents and I learned to cope with our scars. We did not permit them to spoil our new life. Suffering had taught us to appreciate even the little things in life. We take nothing for granted; especially our freedom. It is much like taking medicine to alleviate pain. When the effects of the painkiller wears off, the pain comes back. Our lives have fragile boundaries between comfort and pain. The images of the past are easily triggered by common stimuli: the sound of a train, certain smells, and the sight of smoke-stacks. There is almost no day that I am not reminded of the past. But, I no longer have nightmares. The clear-cut images and painfully accurate memories are becoming slightly more faint now. I am afraid that with the passage of time, they will become as faded photographs, and I feel guilty because I may be capable of glossing over the absolute horror and degradation. Today, Revisionists would like to re-write history and omit The Holocaust. If the survivors of it cannot remember and warn, then there never was a Holocaust. I live with a dual personality. I want to forget the past, yet I want to hold on to it because of the importance of memory and the lesson for the future."

The bell rings to announce the end of the period. The principal thanks me for coming, and the children applaud; showing their approval. A stream of children come over to me before taking leave. The tall Black boy, who had asked some questions is the first to approach me. "May I give you a hug?" he asks. I take him in my arms and give him a kiss on his forehead. The others follow. I am besieged by hugs and handshakes. One Oriental girl speaks to me with a heavy Chinese accent, "I'm so glad you are alive." Tears fill my eyes. The auditorium is suddenly empty. I walk out of the school into the sunlight, the child's words repeating in my head. "I'm so glad you are alive! I'm so glad you are alive."...

The message Mrs. Smith, my former home-bound teacher, wrote in my memory book suddenly jumps into mind: "Hitch your wagon to a star." Yes, I tried to leave the yellow star of death behind, and hitched myself to the star of life.

The Nazis subjected me to suffering and degradation, which ultimately led to a weakened body, and the ravages of disease by a potentially deadly microscopic organism. But, despite the odds, I survived because of a strong will, faith in God, determination and hard work. Seizing the opportunities that the land of the free and the home of the brave offered, I have found a fulfilling life in America, a life beyond the yellow star.

Inge speaking in a classroom.
From "Daily News."

Inge and doll, Marlene.

ABOUT THE AUTHOR

Inge Auerbacher was born in Kippenheim, Germany. She was imprisoned from 1942 to 1945 in the Terezin concentration camp in Czechoslovakia when she was seven to ten years of age. In 1946 she emigrated to the United States of America and has lived in New York City since then.

Ms. Auerbacher graduated from Queens College with a B.S. degree in chemistry and has done post-graduate work in biochemistry at Hunter College. She has been associated with many renowned researchers in the field of medicine. Today, she is a chemist for Mount Sinai Services at City Hospital Center in Elmhurst.

A world traveler, travel writer, and avid photographer, Ms. Auerbacher is also a poet with more than fifty poems published. She wrote the lyrics to "We Shall Never Forget," the only original song presented at the World Gathering of Jewish Holocaust Survivors, 1981, in Jerusalem. The lyrics are set to music composed by Rosalie Commentucci-O'Hara. The record album, *Jewish Memories*, contain four of Ms. Auerbacher's lyrics, sung by the cantor and entertainer Sol Zim. Other lyrics have been set to music by James Donenfeld and Barney Bragin.

I Am A Star—Child Of The Holocaust, Ms. Auerbacher's award-winning autobiography of her early childhood and her years spent in the Terezin concentration camp has been published in many languages.

In 1985, Inge Auerbacher appeared in *Childhood Memories of the Holocaust*, a television documentary produced by the New York City Board of Education.

She was the subject of the documentary films *Inge and the Yellow Star* and *All Jews Out*, produced in Germany. Both films were shown on German television. *All Jews Out* has been presented in many countries and has won prizes at major film festivals.

Ms. Auerbacher spends much of her free time lecturing on the Holocaust.

REVIEWS

Inge Auerbacher's second narrative—about the miraculous rebirth of hope in the heart of Jewish children—is as absorbing and as moving as her first testimony. I highly recommend it.

—Elie Wiesel
Andrew W. Mellon Professor in the Humanities
at Boston University, and Nobel Prize Winner

In today's world, young adults are surrounded by a sea of violence. Daily, the news media floods their reading and listening materials with reports of the civil war in Africa's Rwanda; the "ethnic-cleansing" and slaughters in the former Yugoslavia; the continued violence between Northern Ireland and England battling over land each wants to claim; the attempted annihilation of Kurds in hostile Iraq where the Kurds suffer gassings, burnings and killings! Inge Auerbacher brings a story of hope "against all odds" to its readers young and old. Her story of courage during Hitler's Nazis attempted annihilation of all Europe's Jews will give determination to the young. Ms. Auerbacher's struggles here in America after her liberation from the death camps will give our young adults a ray of hope not despair in today's sea of violence here and abroad. I personally congratulate Inge Auerbacher for bearing her soul in her struggles in Europe and America. Her life is an example of moral courage, tolerance, acceptance, and respect for all peoples regardless of race, color, creed, sex or sexual orientation. The book *Beyond The Yellow Star To America* must be required reading, especially, for all high school students—many who now are requested by their state education departments to not only study the Holocaust but also to be leaders in our pluralist America. This book, a profile of undaunted courage, I prophesy has profound material for an excellent film.

—Sister Rose Thering, O.P., Ph.D.
Executive Director
National Christian Leadership Conference for Israel

I read your *Beyond the Yellow Star To America* with great interest. I learned a great deal about your background and ordeal both during and after the war. I was greatly impressed with the way you dealt with the many personal, physical, and emotional blows you suffered during the first decades of your life. Your defiance of the enemy—you survived in spite of the Nazis' commitment to destroy every Jew, your mature physical and emotional reactions to a dreadful disease, and above all, your commitment to bear witness constitute an inspirational story that will surely move the readers of your autobiography. I will not hesitate to recommend it as a solid, highly readable account.

— Randolph L. Braham
Distinguished Professor Emeritus
The Rosenthal Institute for Holocaust Studies
The Graduate School and University Center of
The City University of New York

It is suspenseful and interesting. It is fascinating for adults and adolescents, a significant contribution to the Holocaust literature.

—Judith S. Kestenberg, M.D.
Co-director of the International
Study of Organized Persecution of Children

Elie Wiesel and Inge. State Department Luncheon at opening of The United States Holocaust Memorial Museum, Washington, D.C., 1993.

As Holocaust survivors, Inge and I were on the same boat that took us to the brightness of America. I applaud her strength and resolve to make a new life. Her story is one of courage and overcoming great odds without harboring bitterness.

This book should inspire all and should be read by everyone.

— Benjamin Meed
President, American Gathering/
Federation of Jewish Holocaust Survivors

Finally, here is a much needed book in the social science and psychology literature for adolescents and more mature readers. Not only will readers learn about a "survivor" and her place in the scheme of history, but they will also identify with Inge's teenage insecurities and needs in a non-war zone, contemporary setting. The scars, the healing and the drive to taking control of her life will readily be understood. The well-written autobiography is fast-paced and its wealth of pictures makes it a fine resource for organizations and programs dealing with overcoming prejudice; integration; self-esteem; brotherhood.

—Myrna Kemnitz
Director (Ret.), ESEA Program